The Torch of True Meaning

བཀའ་ཆེན་ཁ་ཁྲིགས་ཁྱིར་ཙྩེ་ཀ་ཡེ།

The Torch of True Meaning

Instructions and the Practice Text for the Mahamudra Preliminaries

Jamgön Kongtrul Lodrö Thaye
and the Ninth Karmapa Wangchuk Dorje

Foreword by
His Holiness the Seventeenth Karmapa
Ogyen Trinley Dorje

KTD Publications, Woodstock, New York
Kagyu Monlam, Bodhgaya, India

Copublished by KTD Publications and the Kagyu Monlam

KTD Publications
335 Meads Mountain Road
Woodstock, NY 12498 USA
ktdpublications@kagyu.org
www.KTDPublications.com

Kagyu Monlam
Sujata Bypass
Bodhgaya, 823231 Gaya, Bihar, India

ISBN 978-1-934608-52-4

Printed in the USA on 100% PCR, acid-free paper.

Contents

The Karmapa

Foreword

Often people wonder whether a particular Dharma practice belongs to the Mahayana or to the Foundation vehicle. Yet it is not really a question of whether the practice is Mahayana or Foundation vehicle—the label it is given does not make it one or the other. Instead, it depends upon the resolve of the practitioner: if their motivation is bodhichitta, then it becomes Mahayana. But if it is a Foundation vehicle motivation, the practice becomes a Foundation vehicle practice. People might think that it is the practice that is the Great Perfection, but that is not how it is. What is important is not that the practice be the Great Perfection but that the individual must become the Great Perfection.

Similarly, many people, when they hear of the highest stages of Dharma study and practice, such as "emptiness" or "mahamudra", want to study or practice them immediately. However, without a stable foundation, which is the essential prerequisite to such advanced practices, even if they were to study or practice them, they would not be able to experience their profundity.

This is the reason why *The Torch of True Meaning* is such an important text. Composed by the first Jamgön Kongtrul Lodrö Thaye, it gives comprehensive instructions on how to practice the ngöndro, the essential preparation for all practitioners before beginning mahamudra. Anyone who wishes to practice the ngöndro of the Kagyu lineage and in particular the Karma Kagyu lineage should first read this text carefully and internalize its meaning. They will then have a stable ground for the practice of mahamudra. This is not just the correct way to practice, but also the most beneficial.

Even though previous translations of *The Torch of True Meaning* have helped many, David Karma Choephel has worked hard to retranslate it into a more modern style and bring it closer to the original meaning. I have also made a few, small efforts as a contribution to this process.

I am very happy that this translation is to be published jointly by KTD Publications and the Kagyu Monlam, and will be available for distribution on a donation basis to all who wish to practice the four preliminaries. I would also like to thank everyone involved in this translation. I hope it will bring benefit to all who read it.

17th Karmapa Ogyen Trinley Dorje,
Himachal Pradesh, India,

9th August, 2014

Foreword by His Holiness the Seventeenth Gyalwang Karmapa Ogyen Trinley Dorje

Often people wonder whether a particular Dharma practice belongs to the Mahayana or to the Foundation vehicle. Yet it is not really a question of whether the practice is Mahayana or Foundation vehicle—the label it is given does not make it one or the other. Instead, it depends upon the resolve of the practitioner: if their motivation is bodhichitta, then it becomes Mahayana. But if it is a Foundation vehicle motivation, the practice becomes a Foundation vehicle practice. People might think that it is the practice that is the Great Perfection, but that is not how it is. What is important is not that the practice be the Great Perfection but that the individual must become the Great Perfection.

Similarly, many people, when they hear of the highest stages of Dharma study and practice, such as "emptiness" or "mahamudra" want to study or practice them immediately. However, without a stable foundation, which is the essential prerequisite to such advanced practices, even if they were to study or practice them, they would not be able to experience their profundity.

This is the reason why *The Torch of True Meaning* is such an important text. Composed by the first Jamgön Kongtrul Lodrö Thaye, it gives comprehensive instructions on how to practice the ngöndro, the essential preparation for all practitioners before beginning mahamudra.

Anyone who wishes to practice the ngöndro of the Kagyu lineage and in particular the Karma Kagyu lineage should first read this text carefully and internalize its meaning. They will then have a stable ground for the practice of mahamudra. This is not just the correct way to practice, but also the most beneficial.

Even though previous translations of *The Torch of True Meaning* have helped many, David Karma Choephel has worked hard to retranslate it into a more modern style and bring it closer to the original meaning. I have also made a few, small efforts as a contribution to this process.

I am very happy that this translation is to be published jointly by KTD Publications and the Kagyu Monlam, and will be available for distribution on a donation basis to all who wish to practice the four preliminaries. I would also like to thank everyone involved in this translation. I hope it will bring benefit to all who read it.

17th Karmapa Ogyen Trinley Dorje,
Himachal Pradesh, India,
9th September, 2014

Translator's Introduction

For many who come to the practice of Tibetan Buddhism in general and mahamudra in particular, the preliminary ngöndro practices are like a rite of passage, deepening their commitment to the practice of meditation. And this book *The Torch of True Meaning* is an indispensable guide for that process, especially in the Karma Kagyu tradition. The original, pioneering translation by Judith Hanson has been available (under the title *The Torch of Certainty*) for many years now, and many have relied on it for inspiration and advice. But His Holiness the Gyalwang Karmapa Ogyen Trinley Dorje thought a new edition would be helpful and asked me to prepare this translation for publication.

The author of *The Torch of True Meaning*, Jamgön Kongtrul Lodrö Thaye (1813–1899), was one of the leaders of the nonsectarian Rimé movement that led to a resurgence of the Dharma throughout Tibet but especially in its eastern parts. His great talents were recognized while he was still young, and he was named a tulku (reincarnate lama) in spite of not actually being one in order to prevent him being put to secular service for the king. Though he is associated as a main lineage holder of the Karma Kamtsang, he received teachings from all the different lineages that had spread to Tibet and taught, wrote about, and spread them all. In particular, he sought out rare teachings and preserved the lineages of empowerments, transmission, and instructions that otherwise would have been lost. He compiled all these teachings in what are called his *Five Great Treasuries* and also wrote many commentaries, meditation instructions, and other texts himself—his complete oeuvre including the *Five Great Treasuries* fills well over a hundred volumes. Yet he was not merely a scholar and author; he was also a great meditation master who spent decades in solitary retreat, and his own experience in meditation flavors all of his works—perhaps this *Torch of True Meaning* most especially.

Written primarily for meditators, *The Torch* is forthright and easy to understand. On the outermost level, it reflects the lifestyle of premodern Tibet in many ways: Jamgön Kongtrul uses the things people would see in their lives as farmers or nomads for examples, and frequently refers to types of spirits such as *döns* and *bhutas* that have no direct equivalent in the bestiaries of the Western spirit world. It was written during a time when the fragility of life was more evident than it is in the antiseptic developed world of the twenty-first century, in a context where most people would have had many friends and family members who perished early from infection, disease, accident, or violence. But the underlying meaning of the text holds as true now as it did then, and the practice of mahamudra still requires that we appreciate the preciousness of a human body, take our mortality to heart, feel deep revulsion for samsara, purify our beings, gather the accumulations, and most of all develop heartfelt devotion for the master who can guide us to see our true nature as it is. Jamgön Kongtrul clearly explains here what we need to do ourselves in order to achieve just that.

The Torch is paired here with a new translation of the liturgy for the Karma Kamtsang preliminary practices, by the Ninth Karmapa Wangchuk Dorje. There are several translations and editions of this practice already available, and Jamgön Kongtrul's commentary can be used with any of them. This version, however, is based on a Tibetan text prepared by His Holiness the Karmapa. It is essentially the same as the other available editions except that the lineage supplication in the guru yoga has been edited and shortened, and a few other edits have been made as well. Just as the original was largely compiled from preexisting practice texts, I have largely assembled the translation from other texts I had translated previously for the Kagyu Monlam or from other practices.

When the Dharma was translated into Tibetan, Tibetan translators worked together with Indian panditas with whom they confirmed every word of their translations, but present-day translators into English rarely get a similar opportunity. I was fortunate enough to do the bulk of the translation while staying near the Karmapa, and His Holiness answered many of my questions at that time. Later he also reviewed the entire translation of *The Torch*, making many changes and suggestions. If this translation is of benefit, it is primarily due to his kindness, patience, and clarity in explaining things to me.

I did not start this translation with a blank slate; I relied heavily on an earlier translation by Lama Willa Miller, and many of her words remain in the final translation. I am grateful for her initial generosity in sharing her work as well as for her graciousness throughout this process. Additionally, Lama Eric Triebelhorn took the time to thoroughly review a draft and made dozens of corrections and suggestions, and Jo Gibson gave invaluable input during the editing. I am thankful to them and to everyone else who helped in other ways as well, for without their contributions, this translation would not have been worth reading.

In spite of all the help I have received from His Holiness and many others, it is still possible that there are mistakes, inadequacies, and inconsistencies remaining in this translation. These are all my own responsibility, and I would like to beg the reader's pardon for them. I hope that all those who read this book may take its meaning to heart and be inspired to do whatever they can in this life to bring themselves and others the lasting benefits of mahamudra.

—DKC

Phyag chen sngon 'gro bzhi sbyor dang dngos
gzhi'i khrid rim mdor bsdus nges don sgron
me zhes bya ba bzhugs so//

The Concise Graduated Instructions
on the Four Preliminaries and
Main Practice of Mahamudra

པད་ཆེན་པོ་ལ་ཀོ་རྩེ་ཀ་ལེ།

The Torch of True Meaning

The Four Ordinary Preliminaries

I bow my head to Varjadhara Pema Nyinche Wangpo,
Who upholds the lineage of the wish-fulfilling jewels,
Glorious Dusum Khyenpa's oral transmission passed down
From the forebears of all siddhas, Marpa, Mila, and Gampopa.

Perfect, supreme Buddha, accept me
And all sentient beings as your followers
In this and all our lifetimes, and bless us
So that we realize the true nature.

We have all been born human. We need to understand that the significance of entering the gate of Dharma is that our minds must move toward the Dharma. In order for this to occur, we must know the qualities of the Three Jewels and have the faith of conviction. But if we do not recall death and impermanence, that faith will not serve as a solid basis, and for that reason we must first meditate on impermanence. Appreciation of impermanence arises due to understanding how difficult it is to gain the leisures and resources of a precious human existence.

[1. The Precious Human Life]

From the root text for the four common preliminaries:

[First meditate on this precious human body
So difficult to gain, so easy to lose.
This time I shall make it meaningful!]

First, meditate as follows: This human body with the eight leisures and ten resources is superior to even a wish-fulfilling jewel because we have not been born in any of the eight states that lack leisure. Contemplate the reasons why it is so difficult to gain.

1. Hell beings experience the sufferings of heat and cold without the slightest break.
2. Hungry ghosts are tormented solely by the sufferings of hunger and thirst.
3. Animals are dull and ignorant and do not understand or know anything.
4. The lands where Buddhism has spread are small and the places where it has not are exceedingly numerous. Those born in outlying lands do not hear even a word of Dharma.
5. Long-lived gods of the Desire, Form, and Formless realms are so distracted by attachment to sensory pleasures and samadhi that they have no interest in the Dharma.
6. Those who have extreme views and those who naturally dislike the Dharma have wrong views.

7. Those in desolate worlds are beings of dark aeons when no
   Buddha has come and not even the words for the Three
   Jewels are heard.
8. The dumb, called *lenpa* in Kham dialect, are idiots whose minds
   do not turn toward the Dharma.

These beings have no opportunity to practice Dharma and are tormented by their particular kind of karma, so they do not have leisure. Right
now, since your mental continuum has not taken birth in any of those
eight unfavorable states, you possess the eight leisures.

Even if you attain a body capable of practicing Dharma, in order to
practice purely, you must not be affected by the sixteen circumstances
without leisure. There are eight defects based on present circumstances:

1. The five poisons being exceedingly coarse and disturbing
   your mind
2. Being influenced by negative companions
3. Having erroneous views and conduct
4. Being extremely lazy
5. Being flooded by obstacles arising from the awakening of previous
   negative actions
6. Being under someone else's control, such as being enslaved or
   indentured
7. Entering the Dharma just to get food and clothing or out of fear
   of death and then acting contrary to the teachings
8. Simulating Dharma practice for sake of offerings, respect,
   and renown

There are eight mental conditions unfavorable to Dharma practice:

1. Having great attachment to your body, possessions, and so forth
2. Behaving badly due to an extremely coarse disposition
3. Not fearing the miseries of samsara and the lower realms, no
   matter how much they are explained

4. Lacking faith, no matter how much the benefits of liberation are taught
5. Being naturally fond of unvirtuous activities
6. Being as interested in Dharma as a dog is in grass
7. Violating bodhichitta and the root vows
8. Violating the samaya you hold with your guru or companions

These sixteen prevent Dharma from arising in your being and are the basis for going to the lower realms, so rejoice that they have not contaminated your being in the past, and train in methods to prevent them from arising in the future.

There are five internal resources:

1. You have obtained a precious human body that is the opposite of the eight states that lack leisure.
2. You have been born in a central country (in terms of Dharma) where Dharma has spread[I].
3. Since your eyes and other sense faculties are intact, you can understand whatever you are taught.
4. Since you have not encountered wrong views and have entered the fold of the Buddha's teachings, you do not have a wrong livelihood.
5. Since you trust the Three Jewels that are the source of refuge, you have faith.

There are five external resources:

1. Although many universes are formed and destroyed, it is difficult for a Buddha to appear even once. However Shakyamuni Buddha has appeared in this age.
2. Pratyekabuddhas and so forth do not teach Dharma even when they appear. However now the Buddha has taught the profound and vast True Dharma.

3. The teachings have remained until now without waning

4. There are many followers of the teachings.

5. Dharma practitioners are not deprived of a Dharmic livelihood because other sentient beings who have renunciation due to illness, aging, and so forth are sympathetic to them and give them food, clothing, and necessities.

In total, there are ten resources, and you possess them.

All sentient beings naturally do wrong acts, and very few act virtuously. Even among virtues, the ability to maintain the discipline necessary to achieve a human body is extremely difficult. For this reason, beings in the three lower realms are as numerous as the atoms in the earth while gods and human beings are exceedingly few. And among them, a human body capable of practicing Dharma is scarcely attainable. For example, we cannot count the number of insects underneath a single flat rock, but it is possible to count all the people living in one country. Yet only a fraction of them practice Dharma, and among them, those who practice it properly are as rare as stars in the daytime.[2]

We never know when this body will perish from fire, water, poison, weapons, strokes, lightning, a fall into a ravine, or so forth. The causes of death are many, and the conditions sustaining life are few. Since the only difference between life and death is just the breath wheezing in and out, this body perishes even more easily than a water bubble.

Therefore you will never obtain a precious human body like this again. Do not dare to waste it. If you were born in an animal body, forget about attaining enlightenment, you would not be capable of reciting even a single *mani*. Additionally, you would automatically accumulate many causes for being reborn in the lower realms.

Because of this body, we are able to achieve even perfect buddhahood, so it has a great purpose. Yet till now, we have squandered it without much point. Worldly people are able to work so hard at farming and so forth in the short term with their eye on the long term, but we cannot

muster even an ounce of endurance or fortitude when it comes to working for what we have wished for in every lifetime. We are rotten to the
core, fickle, and fooled by the maras. Meditate on this again and again,
thinking, "From this day onward, there's no way I won't put all of my
energy into practicing the True Dharma to make this life meaningful."

Generally, when we have not completed an action, it is called unfinished business. Due to unfinished business from our past lives' Dharma
practice, in this life as well we will have faith in the Dharma and guru
we are used to, and we will train under them. This is a sign of the awakening of positive karma. However becoming habituated to wrongdoing
now only creates unfinished business for the lower realms in the next
lifetime—we will not attain a human body again. The *Kshitigarbha
Sutra* states:

> There are ten kinds of individuals in samsara who are unlikely
> to be reborn in a human form. Who are they? They are those
> who have not generated the roots of virtue, who do not accu-
> mulate merit, who are influenced by negative friends, whose
> afflictions continuously propagate themselves, who are not
> afraid of the sufferings of future lives, whose minds are agitated
> by the afflicted, who constantly forget Dharma because of lazi-
> ness and distraction, who embrace the Buddha's teachings but
> do not follow them, who follow wrong views, and who cling to
> wrong views tightly.

Be careful of those.

You should not think that just because you have such a meaningful
human body you are great, you are learned, you are of a high class, or
you are venerable, and then belittle others—it is not appropriate to disparage even a tiny insect, because all beings have buddha nature. It is
said that disparaging others ripens in this life as losing what you value
and in the next as rebirth as a hungry ghost. Even if you are born

human, you will be a slave. Furthermore, ordinary beings lack clairvoyance and thus never know where or in what manner noble beings or bodhisattvas might appear, or how they might act to benefit beings. Therefore never judge others. It is taught that disparaging a bodhisattva results in enduring the misery of hell for many aeons. Thus you must never go too far even as a joke or as a tease.

Individuals with human bodies may have greater or lesser faith, and there are stronger and weaker remedies. Those whose intelligence is limited, who are easily influenced by companions, and who are frightened by the profound words and meaning are the gradual type of individuals. They should remain close to a skillful guru and train in the path in stages, gathering the two accumulations in union, and not be introduced to the view and meditation too early. The instantaneous type of individuals have sharper intelligence, greater compassion, unwavering faith and longing, and little fixation or attachment. They think only of Dharma and feel a special joy for the profound words and meaning. They need not be taught the path of various means and visualization but can be immediately given an introduction to the meaning. I offer this as an aside.

2. Meditation on Impermanence

[Second, the world and living beings are transient,
Especially my life, like a water bubble—
Who knows when I will die and become a corpse?
Since Dharma will help then, I'll practice diligently.]

There are five root verses from the Kadampa school:

1. First, reflect that nothing lasts—everything changes.

The universe is first formed, then remains, and is finally destroyed by
fire and water so that not even a speck of ash is left. Last year, this year,
yesterday, today, and so forth—months and years disappear moment by
moment. All the beings inhabiting this world are also impermanent.
Meditate thinking, "I was like that when I was a baby. Then I was like
that as a child and like that as youth. Now I have aged this much. With
each day and every month, death draws closer and closer—it is nearly
upon me. What would be best? How can I do it?"

2. Contemplate the many others who have died.

Contemplate, thinking, "The people I remember who have died up to
now outnumber those alive now who are older, younger, or the same age
as me. This person lived here, but has died. That was over there, but
now it has fallen into ruins. Only a few die of old age. Most, without
time to think or remember, are suddenly snatched away even at happy
and joyous times. That is how it is. Some who have not died have gone

from high to low, from low to high, from beggar to rich, from rich to destitute. No one I have seen or heard of is beyond impermanence. When will it happen to me as well? Now, while I still have a little time, I must be diligent about practicing the True Dharma."

3. Contemplate the many causes of death again and again.

Meditate intensely, thinking, "Falling rocks, collapsing buildings, lightning, seizures, unbearable abdominal pain, and so forth—there are so many causes of death that we do not know how it will come. We do not know when it will come. If it is karma, there is no way to prevent it. I don't even know whether my food, wealth, clothing, friends, associates, servants, and so forth will become causes of death. The time of death is uncertain, so what will happen to me even now?"

The *Bodhisattvapiṭaka* mentions nine causes of sudden death: Eating food that disagrees with you, overeating when already full, eating before the last meal has digested, not urinating or defecating in a timely manner, patients not heeding the advice of doctors and nurses, being struck by virulent *döns*, taking the wrong emetic, impulsive violent behavior, and engaging in sexual intercourse carelessly. Be wary of these.

4. Contemplate what will happen at the time of death.

Death comes upon us unwanted—we do not accept it willingly. Wicked individuals and those who have previously committed bad acts have the agony of the channels being severed and the terrifying feeling of life ceasing in particular.[3] They experience many mistaken, confused appearances. They lose control of their bodies and minds, so there is no telling what they might think of. The state of the mind at the time of death is so potent that if even a mildly unvirtuous thought arises, rebirth in the lower realms is certain. As that state of mind depends upon our present conditioning, we must start now to habituate ourselves to the Dharma. It goes without saying that divinations, *toh*,[4] medical treatment, healing rites, food, wealth, and so forth cannot fool death—even the power of a buddha cannot bring back a life that has run out. Thus there is no way to avoid death, so we must act now to ensure we have no regrets when the time comes.

5. Contemplate what happens after death.

Meditate that once you have died, you will not be able to carry a single mouthful of food, a set of clothes, or a single gemstone. You won't even be able to bring along the lowliest servant, even if you are a universal emperor. Your corpse will be wrapped in a shroud and bound with a rope. Everyone will be nauseated just looking at it. After a few days, not even a trace of it will remain. Your mind will be out of control, like a feather blown around by the wind, and you will travel the terrifying passages of the bardo. You will wander unwitting into an unknown next life, pursued by your positive and negative acts. There is no way to leave behind the wrongs you have done. The True Dharma and virtue will help, but if you do not strive to accomplish them now, at that time there will be no one to borrow them from and no one to give them to you.

In summary, there is no other way but to practice Dharma from now on—you must not neglect it. You must integrate it into your being, and in order to integrate it, you must practice. You must gain stability in practice so that you will actually feel joy at the time of death and others will venerate you, saying what a pure practitioner you were.

We say, "So-and-so died! How sad!" or "What a tragedy for that family! *Lama khyen!*"[5] But we are numb to the fact that the same thing will soon happen to us. Though we know we will die someday, we think we won't die for a while. Intellectually we know that the time of death is uncertain, but we do not really take it to heart. Thus all those who are deluded by worldly appearances and act contrary to the Dharma when they meet with adversity have no sense.

So think, "Up to now, more than half of my life has gone by. It is as if the Lord of Death has almost arrived at my door. So I have no time to waste thinking about food, wealth, provisions, clothing, my reputation, and so on." Then measure your actions of body, speech, and mind against the yardstick of Dharma. When others take it easy and lay out their pasts and futures in their minds, think to yourself, "What are they thinking? Aren't they afraid of death? The poor things!" Never be without this sense of urgency.

3. Karmic Cause and Effect

[Third, there is no freedom at the time of death.
In order to gain control over karma,
I'll give up misdeeds and always do virtuous acts.
Thinking thus I'll examine myself every day.]

Karmic cause and effect is the fundamental meaning of all the infinite Dharma teachings given by the Buddha. This topic is so incredibly profound and vast that until one has realized one taste,[6] one will not fully comprehend it. Though ordinary beings cannot fully appreciate it, karmic cause and effect can be roughly summarized thus: Virtuous causes produce pleasant results and unvirtuous causes produce painful results.

There are the causes and results of samsara, and there are the causes and results of liberation. As for the first of these two, in samsara, the root of suffering comes down to accumulating negative acts. That comes down to the afflictions, and those come down to the ignorance of cherishing a self. Ignorance—the delusion that is the root of all afflictions— is the obscure darkness of not knowing where samsara came from; what its nature is; how karmic cause and effect benefit and harm us, and so forth. It is that fleeting thought that we cannot identify something, as if we were imagining a place we had never visited, even if a guru explains it or we come to an intellectual understanding through study and contemplation.

Because of this, we grasp at the lack of a "me" as being me. Due to that, we develop many wrong views such as doubt about the true meaning. Desire based on our own bodies, possessions, and so forth arises, and because of that, pride, envy, and stinginess also occur. Hatred arises based on the "other," and from that come anger, contentiousness, grudges, and so forth. Without those afflictions—the three poisons[7]— it is impossible to accumulate karma. And without karma, its result does not occur, so we must do all we can to eliminate those three roots of wandering in samsara.

To summarize samsaric actions, nonmeritorious acts, which are included within the ten nonvirtues, lead to rebirth in the three lower realms. Meritorious actions—virtues such as generosity that are not accompanied by the intention to achieve nirvana—lead to rebirth in high realms as gods or humans. Unmoving karma—*dhyana* meditation that involves clinging—leads to rebirth in the Form and Formless realms.

In brief, until the imprints of thought have been exhausted, we will continue to accumulate karma, and due to that, it will be impossible to stop the confused perceptions of samsara. Thus those fools who meditate on false emptiness and say, "I don't need to pay attention to action and result—I have realized the nature of mind," are great marauders of the teachings.

There are ten unvirtuous actions. There are three nonvirtues of body:

[1.] Taking life is killing anything intentionally, even something as small as an ant or beetle, since there is no big or small when it comes to life.

[2.] Stealing is taking others' possessions covertly, without them being given.

[3.] Sexual misconduct is engaging in sexual activity in the four wrong manners: with the wrong object (those who have vows, another partner, and so forth), at the wrong time (with pregnant women, the sick, or nursing mothers), at the wrong place (near the guru, in a temple, in a stupa building, and so forth), and in the wrong orifice (the mouth, anus, and so forth).

There are four nonvirtues of speech:

[1.] Lying is consciously saying something untrue.

[2.] Divisive speech is saying disturbing things that are a basis for discord.

[3.] Harsh speech is speaking of others' defects to strike a nerve, such as calling them a thief or a cripple.

[4.] Idle chatter is talking about war, business, or women; singing; dancing; playing; and so forth.

There are three nonvirtues of mind:

[1.] Covetousness is thinking, "If only I had that" about another person's wealth, spouse, reputation, or so forth.

[2.] Malice is being displeased that someone else has happiness or wealth.

[3.] Wrong views are disbelieving in past and future lives, karmic cause and effect, the qualities of the Three Jewels, and so forth.

The full ripening of engaging in these ten nonvirtues and related actions is rebirth in the lower realms. Even if you are born human, they will produce much suffering, such as a short life due to killing, being poor due to stealing, and so forth. Thus never commit them, prevent others from doing them, and regret those you have done.

The opposite of the nonvirtuous actions are the ten virtuous actions:

[1.] Refraining from killing and saving lives

[2.] Not taking what is not given from others and being generous with your own food and wealth

[3.] Maintaining discipline without hypocrisy

[4.] Speaking truthfully

[5.] Reconciling those divided by slander

[6.] Speaking gently

[7. Speaking purposefully][8]

[8.] Rejoicing in the prosperity of others

[9.] Always maintaining an altruistic attitude toward others

[10.] Not criticizing the qualities of any religion or philosophy you hear about and believing the Buddha's words

Do these as much as you are able. Get others to do them as well. Rejoice in those that have been done. The result will be rebirth in the higher realms with a long life and so forth—there are many benefits.

Spending time doing various neutral actions such as walking, standing, sleeping, and sitting, which are neither virtuous nor unvirtuous, does not ripen into good or bad experiences, but it pointlessly wastes this human life. Thus do not fall under the influence of distraction and laziness, and spend your time only practicing virtue with mindfulness and awareness.

Abstain from carelessly committing even the slightest wrong— remember that even a small amount of poison can be fatal. Likewise do not disregard even the slightest virtue—remember that gathering barley grain by grain will fill a basket.

Furthermore, you must secondarily achieve what are known as the eight qualities of the higher realms, as they are the basis for a vast accumulation of merit in future lives:

1. A long life due to giving up harming others
2. A pleasant appearance due to offering lamps and giving away clothing and so forth
3. A high social status due to serving your guru and companions without any pride
4. Prosperity due to giving everything desirable to people who have positive qualities, the sick, the destitute, and so forth
5. Authoritative speech due to only speaking virtuously
6. Great power due to making positive aspirations and presenting offerings to the Three Jewels, your parents, and so forth

7. Being born male due to befriending men and protecting beings from castration[9]

8. Abundant powers due to assisting Dharma activities without expectations

Train in the causes of these qualities.

Therefore once you no longer want to be in samsara, you must train in giving up its cause, nonvirtue. Thus you should practice without hypocrisy the virtues that lead to merit taught here and elsewhere as well as the virtues that lead to liberation—the vows, samayas, and so forth.[10] Do not pull the wool over your own eyes.

The first cause of attaining liberation is maintaining pure discipline grounded in the steadfast intention to emancipate yourself from samsara. Based on that, you will develop the samadhi of a one-pointed mind. This produces the prajna that realizes selflessness through which you can know the universal and specific characteristics of impermanence, suffering, emptiness, and so forth. This purifies previously accumulated obscurations, which will never again be able to produce a result. Thus the suffering of samsara will be exhausted, and you will be able to rest in the nature of the awareness free of extremes. This is called by the name "liberation"—attaining liberation or nirvana does not mean going to some other place or becoming someone different.

In summary, it can only be that virtuous actions result in happiness and unvirtuous actions in suffering—it is impossible it could be the other way around, like planting barley and buckwheat seeds.[11] Acts with a positive intention but negative action (such as killing as an offering to the Jewels, or beating or speaking badly of someone in order to benefit people who are significant to you) and acts negative in intent but positive in application (such as building sacred objects out of a wish for fame, studying out of an urge to compete, or masquerading as a good monk out of fear of embarrassment) are indirectly included among the nonvirtues. If even such acts should be rejected like poison, there is no need to speak of those that are actually unvirtuous.

If you boast of or regret virtues and do not overcome wrongdoing with a remedy such as confession, the acts you have done will ripen only upon you, not anyone else. It is impossible that they be lost or depleted even if aeons have passed. Furthermore, even if trifling at the time of the cause, the deed, karma compounds itself. Thus there is no way to measure what will come of powerful acts such as killing out of strong hatred or saving out of pure altruism the life of a being certain to die. Even the slightest virtues or wrongs we do or say thoughtlessly are multiplied hundreds of thousands of times. But it is impossible for actions committed by others to affect your stream of being if you have not participated in both the intention and preparation. Thus if you are able to live by the Buddha's teachings of cause and effect, doing what is to be done and giving up what must be abandoned, there is no way at all anyone else can send you to the three lower realms no matter how evil they are. Thus in all situations examine only your own faults and expand your pure perception of others. As this is the basis of karma and result,[12] the Kagyu forefathers have advised us to consider it very important.

4. The Defects of Samsara

[Fourth, the places, friends, pleasures, and riches of samsara
Are always stricken with the three sufferings,
Like the last feast before an execution.
Cutting the ties of attachment, I'll strive to reach
   enlightenment.]

For those born in the hot hells, all the mountains and valleys are burning iron blazing with furious flames. The rivers and lakes are molten copper and bronze. From the trees falls a rain of swords and other weapons. Multitudes of carnivorous beasts and ferocious demons kill the hell beings, who do not have the power to rest for even a moment. Such is the suffering in the lowest of the eight hot hells, the Incessant, that even the Buddha did not dare speak of it—were he to tell of it, there would be a danger that the compassionate bodhisattvas might vomit blood and die, he said. For those born in the cold hells, all the mountains and valleys are snow and ice. Bitterly cold winds and storms freeze their bodies, cracking them into pieces. Until their life span of quintillions of years is completed, hell beings die again and again, only to be reborn an instant later in the same place to endure the same agony once again. The suffering in the occasional and neighboring hells is comparable.

Those born as hungry ghosts never find any food or drink at all. The hunger and thirst are so intense that even if they look for pus or mucus they get worn out with exhaustion, unable to find any. They have no clothes, so they burn in the summer and freeze in the winter.

When it rains, they perceive falling sparks burning them. They see water as pus and blood. Flames leap from their dislocated joints. They perceive each other as enemies and constantly beat each other up. They live fifteen thousand human years.

For the animals, those living in the oceans are as numerous as grains in the dregs from brewing beer. They eat one another alive and are constantly tormented by fear, wandering wherever the waves carry them. Those who live dispersed on dry land always fear the approach of an enemy and have no peace of mind. Each kills the other. Those domesticated by humans are hitched to plows, killed for their meat and hides, and so on. In addition to their stupidity and delusion, their suffering of hot and cold is similar to that of the hell beings and hungry ghosts.

The gods of the Desire realm are so distracted by temporary pleasures that their lives fly past without them remembering the Dharma. Seven god-days [13] before they die, the five omens of death appear and they see where they will be reborn in their next lives—the hells and so forth. The suffering of death and downfall is the same as that of a fish on hot sand. When their karma is exhausted, those in the four Form realms and the Formless realms regress from samadhi and eventually fall to lower states.

The demigods naturally harbor a resentful envy towards the splendor of the gods, and engage only in acts of waging war. Their merit is weak and they dislike Dharma, so they always lose the battle; their suffering of being killed is extreme.

As for the suffering in the human realm: 1. First, the suffering of birth is like a chick carried off by a falcon. 2. The suffering of aging is like a mother camel losing her calf. 3. The suffering of illness is like a criminal thrown in a dungeon. 4. The suffering of dying is like a captive dragged off by the executioner.

Each of these has five types of suffering:

[1.   Birth]
a. Since being born is accompanied by extreme pain, birth is suffering.

b. Since it plants the seeds that produce and increase the afflictions, birth is accompanied by negative tendencies.

c. Because old age, sickness and death ensue from being born, birth is the basis for suffering.

d. Because the afflictions gradually develop and their karma is accumulated, birth is the basis for the afflictions.

e. Because it is impermanent, being a single moment, birth then perishes without control and is thus suffering.

[2.] Aging is suffering due to five factors:

a. Fading of the complexion

b. Deterioration of form

c. Loss of strength and ability

d. Deterioration of the sense faculties

e. Loss of possessions

[3.] Illness is suffering:

a. Physical and mental discomfort increase.

b. The body naturally changes.

c. There is no ability to enjoy pleasant things.

d. One is forced to rely on unpleasant things.

e. The loss of life approaches.

[4.] Death is accompanied by:

a. Loss of possessions

b. Loss of power

c. Loss of friends and associates

d. Loss of even one's body

e. Intense feelings of mental discomfort

5. Though we disregard misdeeds, suffering, and slander and undergo great difficulty to acquire food, wealth, reputation, and so forth, things do not turn out as we wish. This is the suffering of not getting what you seek.

6.   We fear the arrival of enemies and thieves. We dread that those more powerful will take our possessions. Wearing the stars as a hat and the frost for boots,[14] we exhaust ourselves with too many activities and work, but fear that we will not finish anything or that it will not turn out well. This is the suffering of not keeping what you have.

7.   We worry about being separated from people from whom we cannot bear to be parted, such as parents, siblings, associates, or students. We fear losing power and possessions. We worry about losing our valuables, making mistakes, being slandered by the envious, and so forth. This is the suffering of being separated from what is dear.

8.   There is the suffering of encountering what we do not want—illness, enemies, lawsuits, punishment by the government, murderous beings, gossip and slander, harm in return for help, treacherous associates, and so forth.

These eight sufferings pertain mostly to human beings.

In brief, there is (1) the suffering of suffering—illness, slander, and so forth in the three lower realms and among gods and humans; (2) the suffering of change—temporary pleasures such as life, possessions, calm abidings, and so forth that seem to be pleasurable yet are fleetingly transient; and (3) the pervasive suffering of formation—the five aggregates of grasping[15] that are the basis or container for the other two sufferings. All the suffering of the three realms arises because of the five aggregates, so nowhere you might be born in samsara, high or low, transcends the nature of the three sufferings.

Therefore even whatever seems to be temporary happiness or prosperity—your home, body, possessions, friends, and associates—is only suffering welling up. Thus it should revolt you deeply, like the food offered to a nauseous person or the feast an executioner gives a prisoner condemned to die. Cut your ties from their roots. Destroy desire from its foundation. You must contemplate how extremely valuable the ben-

efits of liberation—the opposite of those defects—are, and devote yourself to the means for attaining enlightenment.

Generally, these four ordinary preliminaries are found in all the graded
instructions, but this is the peerless Gampopa's supplement to Atisha's
stages of the path for the three types of individuals, merging the streams
of the Kadampa and Mahamudra into one. If you do not apply some
fortitude to these four, then all your meditation on the main practice
will only serve to reinforce the eight worldly concerns.

The root of all Dharma is giving up on this life. But these days, no
Dharma practitioners sever the ties to this life. We do not turn our
minds away from desire. We have not abandoned attachment to relatives, friends, associates, and servants. We have not relinquished even
the slightest desire for food, clothing, and reputation. Thus our spiritual
practice is not effective and our beings are contrary to the Dharma.

We do not consider whether the afflictions have diminished or not
since we started practicing Dharma but count the months and years we
have practiced instead. Rather than examining our own faults, we examine the faults of others. We become conceited about even the smallest
quality. Our minds fall under the sway of personal gain, respect, and
distractions. There are many pointless conversations and things to do.
We think we have integrated the Dharma we practice with the world,
but do not accomplish a single one of our aims. The reason is that we
have not remembered impermanence, so we have become complacent.

The Victorious Drikungpa said, "The preliminaries are even more
profound than the main practice." Thus it would seem far better to
develop these four preliminaries in our beings even the slightest bit than
say we have completed the approach and accomplishment of the four
classes of tantra. Practicing Dharma while letting our minds remain
ordinary only fools ourselves and others and wastes this human life.

In short, if you do not give rise to some degree of renunciation, all your meditation will amount to no more than a pile of manure on a mountainside. So reflect on the sufferings of samsara and the uncertainty of the time of death, and focus on the immediate as much as you can.

It is said that when you begin to practice the Dharma, the maras create obstacles and your faith can diminish. Signs of being possessed by the maras include perceiving faults in your spiritual friend the guru, perceiving faults in Dharma practitioners in general, associating with ordinary friends, losing diligence in your practice, indulging in sensory pleasures, and having no devotion to the Three Jewels. Thus you should contemplate the qualities of the guru and the Three Jewels and develop pure perception of other Dharma practitioners. Seeing another person as bad is a sign of your own impure karma—remember the analogy of seeing your grimy face in a mirror. Do not keep company with ordinary people. Do not heed their words. Reflect on the defects of sensory pleasures.

In general, without faith no positive qualities at all will arise, so faith must precede all Dharma practice. There are many types of faith, but conviction and heartfelt dedication encompass them all. The conditions that produce faith are the vicissitudes of the transmigration of birth and death, illness, *döns*, and adverse conditions, as well as reading the biographies of great masters of the past and the stories of the Buddha's previous lives. You should engender faith by reflecting on these each and every day.

Some people seem to have extremely strong faith when they are with the guru but forget it when apart. Some have faith when they encounter adversity but lose it later. Some have strong faith when they receive the Dharma or material things they wanted, or when they are overcome by illness, *döns*, and so forth, but lack it afterwards. Lacking firm, heart-felt faith for a single root guru and a single profound teaching, they set aside one and take up the next they become infatuated with. Reject such behavior and with stable, immutable faith, do not turn your attention outside and please do some practice internally instead. Then when each small quality of the Dharma dawns in your being, you will understand the profundity of this special instruction. This produces certainty in the Dharma. At this point, you will remember the kindness of the guru and devotion will naturally develop. Through this, all the qualities of the path will effortlessly and spontaneously arise.

The Four Uncommon Preliminaries

1. Going for Refuge

The first of the four uncommon preliminaries is going for refuge. For the visualization: The place is a spacious and vast pure realm whose ground yields when pressed and springs back when released. In the middle of a lush, green meadow covered with abundant flowers is a lake whose waters have the eight qualities. The lake is filled with many divine birds warbling with lovely calls. In the center of the lake is a wish-fulfilling tree made of precious jewels and bowed down with leaves, fruit, and flowers made of precious jewels. Like a parasol, from a single trunk four branches extend in the four directions and a fifth extends up.

At the center of the middle branch is a jeweled throne supported by eight lions and covered with priceless cloths made of divine fabrics. On top of these is a thousand-petaled lotus and full-moon seat. In the middle of this sits Vajradhara, your root guru in essence, who is deep blue like the autumn sky. He has one face and two arms. His hands are crossed at his heart; his right holds a golden vajra and his left a silver bell.[16] His gaze peaceful, he is replete with the thirteen peaceful ornaments—a diadem, earrings, and so forth.[17] His upper garment is made of multicolored silk, and he wears a red lower garment. He is seated in the vajra posture,[18] and his body, adorned with the marks and signs,[19] glows brilliantly. He regards you with great joy.

In a column above the crown of Vajradhara's head in ascending order are Pema Nyinche Wangpo, Mipham Chödrup Gyatso, Düdül Dorje, Chökyi Jungne, Jangchub Dorje, Chökyi Döndrup, Yeshe Dorje, Yeshe Nyingpo, Chöying Dorje, Chökyi Wangchuk, Wangchuk Dorje,

Könchok Yenlak, Mikyö Dorje, Sangye Nyenpa, Chödrak Gyatso, Paljor Döndrup, Jampal Sangpo, Tongwa Dönden, Rikpay Raldri, Deshin Shekpa, Kachö Wangpo, Rolpay Dorje, Yungtön Dorje Pal, Rangjung Dorje, Orgyen Rinpoche Pal, Drupchen Pakshi, Pomdrak Sonam Dorje, Drogön Rechen Sangye Drak, Dusum Khyenpa, Peerless Gampopa, Jetsün Mila, Marpa the Translator, Maitripa, Shavari, Noble Nagarjuna, Saraha, Lodro Rinchen, and Vajradhara.[20]

In the space surrounding them, amassed like clouds, are the six ornaments of this world,[21] Telopa, Naropa, and the learned and accomplished gurus from India and Tibet such as the Drikung, Drukpa, Tsalpa, and Taklung lineages, and so forth.

On the eastern branch, on lotus, sun, and corpse seat is Vajra Varahi surrounded by hosts of yidam deities of the four or six classes of tantra: Chakrasamvara, Hevajra, and Guhyasamaja; Mahamaya, Buddha Kapala, and Vajra Catuhpitha; Krishna Yamari, Shan Mukha, and Vajra Bhairava; as well as Kalachakra, and so forth.

On the right branch, on a lion throne, lotus and moon seat, is our teacher Shakyamuni, surrounded by the thousand Buddhas of this fortunate aeon and all the Buddhas of the ten directions and three times.

On the rear branch are the twelve types of scriptures of the True Dharma,[22] in particular the Mahayana sutras and the tantras of the secret mantra, in the form of volumes with golden labels pointing toward you, murmuring with the natural sound of the ĀLI AND KĀLI.

On the left branch are the sanghas of the Foundation and Greater vehicles, countless bodhisattvas, arhats, and pratyekabuddhas including the three lords of the families and the rest of the eight close sons, the bodhisattvas of the fortunate aeon, the excellent pair, Ananda, the sixteen arhats, and so forth.[23]

In the space below the branches are, principally, Dorje Bernakchen, Palden Lhamo, Four-Armed Mahakala, and Six-Armed Mahakala among an inconceivable number of the wisdom protectors, heroes, dakinis, and so forth.

You are on the ground in front of the sources of refuge with your own father to your right and your own mother to your left, the foremost among all sentient beings who fill the reaches of space. In particular there are the enemies who hate you, harmful obstructive spirits, beings with whom you have had feuds and karmic debs from beginningless time, tormented ghosts, döns, and *bhutas* gathered in throngs. Think that with you as their leader, all of them pay respect with their bodies by joining their palms, respect with their minds through faith and longing, and respect with their speech by reciting the refuge prayer in a sonorous rumble. Imagining this, recite the refuge prayer one hundred or one thousand times without your mind wandering elsewhere and while contemplating the meaning of the words. At the end, give rise to bodhichitta. Then, the sources of refuge along with their seats, thrones and so forth melt into light and dissolve into you. Think that their bodies, speech, and minds become inseparable from your body, speech, and mind, and let your mind rest naturally. Dedicate the merit.

To explain a bit about the meaning of going for refuge, in the world, when we fear the approach of a danger such as a violent person or so forth, we seek a guardian or refuge who can protect us. Likewise innumerable perils of various kinds constantly threaten us in this life, the next, and in the bardo as we sink in the ocean of samsaric suffering with no occasion for liberation. No one—not our parents, relatives, friends, powerful gods, or nagas—can protect us from them, nor can we avert them on our own. Thus we have no choice but to seek a refuge. No one but the Three Jewels is able to guide us out of samsara, and we must gain freedom ourselves to be able to protect others.

"Three Jewels" means the Buddha, the Dharma, and the Sangha. In the mantra tradition, you should also add the three roots: the root of blessing is the guru, the root of accomplishment is the yidam, and the root of activity is the dakinis and Dharma protectors. In the mantra tradition, it is said that these three roots are also included within the Three Jewels, and furthermore, all of them are embodied in your root guru alone.

The Buddha encompasses the three bodies: the dharmakaya that knows the nature and variety of all phenomena; the sambhogakaya with the five certainties, and the created, incarnate, and supreme nirmanakayas.[24] The Dharma is comprised of both scripture and realization. Scriptural Dharma is the scriptures in the form of names, words, and letters and of that which is verbally spoken. The Dharma of realization is the ground, the dharma expanse of suchness; the result, the truth of cessation; and the truth of the path, the factors of enlightenment. The actual Sangha is the irreversible bodhisattvas, and the provisional is the noble listeners and pratyekabuddhas.

The Buddha is the one who shows us what to adopt and what to abandon, so take the Buddha as the teacher. What he taught is what we are to practice, so take the Dharma as the path. We must practice according to the transmission of the instructions, practice, and deeds of the noble beings, who are like guides on an unknown path. Thus we take the Sangha as our companions. When we come to the end of the path, a separate Dharma and Sangha are not necessary, and they become one with the buddhas' wisdom minds. Thus the ultimate refuge is the Buddha alone.

In the context of philosophy, there is much talk about how to identify these and what is or is not a source of refuge, but such things are unnecessary for those who only practice or who have instilled virtuous imprints—they should tame their beings with faith and longing as much as they can. As a temporary visual support for engendering faith, sutras speak about "the buddhas in front of you," so statues and stupas are included among the types of buddhas. Implicitly, this means that you should also meditate on the volumes of the sutras and tantras of the True Dharma and the Sangha of ordinary individuals with discipline as the actual Jewels and go to them for refuge with faith and longing.

Going for the refuge of the Foundation vehicle or of the worldly is not going for refuge purely and will not lead to authentic benefit. Therefore it is of utmost importance to think that all sentient beings throughout the reaches of space go for refuge from now until they achieve enlightenment. That makes it Mahayana refuge.

You are going for refuge properly if four factors are present:

1. Knowing the qualities of the Three Jewels according to presentations such as that of *The Sutra of the Recollection of the Three Jewels*
2. Knowing that the Buddha, Dharma, and Sangha are superior to other teachers, mistaken paths, non-Buddhists, and so forth
3. Committing to refuge from the depths of your being due to knowing these points
4. Not seeking refuge in anything but the Three Jewels even at the risk of your life

It is not enough to take refuge by repetition and mouthing words. You must trust the Three Jewels from the core of your being. If you trust in them, the compassion of the Three Jewels will never fail to protect you. It might seem as if the Three Jewels have run out of compassion for those whose bad karma must ripen in this life, but if you trust in faith, they will definitely protect you from the next lifetime on. Saying "The Three Jewels have no compassion!" when the slightest undesirable thing occurs or placing all your hopes in divination, *toh*, and medical treatment is a sign of small-mindedness. If the compassion of the Three Jewels does not seem evident for a time, it is our fault for not supplicating them. It is impossible that the Three Jewels would lack blessings.

Therefore at all times cultivate faith by recollecting the qualities of the Three Jewels, and exert yourself in prayer. Do not engage in negative actions such as idle talk and criticism. Considering all representations of body, speech, and mind and anyone who wears monastic robes to be the actual Three Jewels, prostrate to them, present them with offerings, and have faith and devotion toward them. Restore old statues, texts, and stupas, and create new ones. Do not place such objects on the bare ground or in a place where they might fall. It is inappropriate to even consider selling them for food or pawning them.

Do not step over even a fragment of a small broken sacred image or a single letter of scripture. With gratitude, employ your body, speech, and mind to show them respect through prostrations, offerings, and praise. Recalling their compassion, encourage others to go for refuge and speak of the great qualities of the Three Jewels. Recalling their benefits, go for refuge six times throughout the day and night.[25] Remembering the faults of being without them, never reject them even if your life is at stake. Recollecting your confidence in them, through all your happiness and suffering, all your ups and downs, entrust your mind only to the Three Jewels and do not be disheartened.

In brief, once you have taken refuge in the Buddha, do not worship other worldly gods. Once you have taken refuge in the Dharma, give up thoughts and actions that harm sentient beings. Once you have taken refuge in the Sangha, do not associate with friends who hold extreme views or views that lead to those. If you practice properly, going for refuge alone encompasses most of the stages of the paths of sutra and mantra. If you have not brought the experience of going for refuge into your being, you might spout lofty words about emptiness, but that is the great precipice of the wrong path.

Therefore if you are never separate from the practice of going for refuge, you have entered the ranks of Buddhists. Lesser negative actions will be purified. Larger ones will be lightened and weakened. Humans and nonhumans will be unable to cause you obstacles. Taking refuge causes all roots of virtue, such as vows and chanting, to increase and grow. If you fully trust the Three Jewels, even if you feel yourself driven towards the lower realms, you will not be born there. It says in *The White Lotus Sutra*, "Even those who pretend to be lay and spiritual practitioners who have entered my teachings will pass into nirvana in the expanse without remainder in this fortunate aeon itself—not even one will be left behind." This intends those who have gone for refuge.

Going for refuge has great benefits, but I have only mentioned a few.

The Generation of Bodhichitta Connected with Going for Refuge

Generally, even if a person's mind has moved towards Dharma, whether or not the Dharma becomes the path depends on whether or not they have developed bodhichitta. Whether you engage in slight or great virtue, Dharma is said to have become the path if that virtue has become a means for attaining buddhahood. When embraced by bodhichitta, there is no need to mention virtues—even ordinary activities become means for attaining buddhahood. It says in the sutras, "Those who want to awaken to completely perfect buddhahood should not train in many Dharmas. Train in one. What is that one? Bodhichitta."

There are two types of bodhichitta, relative and ultimate. These two are the root of the 84,000 teachings of the Buddha, so it is difficult to grasp the full extent of their expositions, but much explanation is not necessary here in this context of resting meditation. If you wish to learn more, you should study the six Kadampa treatises and so forth.[26] In brief, the essence of relative bodhichitta is compassion. The essence of ultimate bodhichitta is the prajna that realizes the way things are. These two arise in dependence on each other. Padampa Sangye said, "If compassion has not arisen, realization will not arise. You only find fish in water, not on dry land." Thus based on the relative, the ultimate nature of things is unmistakenly realized. At that time, uncontrived compassion spontaneously wells up for beings who have not realized it, as does the capacity to devote your body, speech, and mind to the benefit of others. Thus at first, when we talk about being embraced by bodhichitta or not, we are speaking about relative bodhichitta, so we must develop that first. Relative bodhichitta has two types—aspirational and engaged—both of which must be engendered through rituals.

There are some superior individuals who develop it by sincerely reciting the words of the bodhisattva vow three times in the presence of a statue of the Buddha. Ordinary beings need to receive the vow from a spiritual friend who holds an unbroken lineage of the bodhisattva vow. In either case, thenceforth one must definitely confess violations and resolve never to commit them again. Best is to confess and resolve six times each day and night; the middling way is to do so at the beginning and end of each of the four sessions; or at the very least, one should recite it once each day and night.

Aspirational bodhichitta is repeatedly meditating, "I will achieve omniscient buddhahood for the sake of all sentient beings." This is analogous to wishing to go somewhere. Engaged bodhichitta is to say to yourself, "To accomplish that end, I will meditate on the oral instructions of coemergent mahamudra" and then engage in accomplishing the virtuous acts you have previously committed to. This is analogous to setting out on the road and going.

In this context, before the dissolution of the sources of refuge, recite the prayer which begins, "Until I reach enlightenment's essence..." three times. Then think to yourself in the presence of that supreme field, "Just as the victors of the past and their children aroused aspirational bodhichitta and then trained in the precepts of engaged bodhichitta, I too, for the sake of my parents—all sentient beings—arouse bodhichitta and will train step-by-step in the trainings, the six transcendences." Then rejoice on your own behalf, meditate that others praise you, and make aspirations. At the end, the sources of refuge dissolve into you.

Normally, when you renew the bodhisattva vow, imagine that in the sky in front of you upon a lion throne, lotus and moon seat is our teacher Shakyamuni surrounded by the eight close sons, sixteen arhats and so forth—the Sanghas of bodhisattvas, listeners, and pratyekabuddhas—and take the vow. At the end, rest without any reference point.

Since all Dharma activities and practices can become precepts of bodhichitta, their scope is extremely vast. But in brief, the precepts of aspirational bodhichitta are that forsaking a sentient being and developing a contrary attitude destroy the vow at its root. Thus once you have taken the bodhisattva vow, it is important to abandon these two. The downfall of forsaking sentient beings is to give up on and get angry at sentient beings—no matter how many or few they are—such as those for whom you harbor grudges, thinking "I won't help you even if I get the chance" out of a motivation of hatred or envy. A contrary attitude is to think, "Someone like me could never benefit myself or others, so it would be better to just be an ordinary worldly person." Or it is to think, "It is too hard to attain perfect Buddhahood, so it does not matter whether I rouse bodhichitta or not." Or to think, "I will never be able to benefit other beings," and develop the resolve of the listeners and pratyekabuddhas focused on your own benefit; to think that bodhichitta doesn't really have much benefit and become relaxed about the vow; and so forth. If more than one session passes without remedying these two with the antidotes, the bodhisattva vow is broken, so from the outset apply mindfulness continually so that they do not occur. Should they arise accidentally, quickly rectify them with confession and resolve.

In brief, never let the excellent attitude of wishing to bring sentient beings—including even malicious enemies and döns—to the level of buddhahood deteriorate. Even the most serious transgressions of a listener, such as the defeats, cannot destroy bodhichitta. Therefore engage in everything you can do to actually be of benefit to others. Even if you are unable to do so now, never be without the intent to help in the long term.

Give up the four negative actions that will cause you to forget bodhichitta in all future lifetimes, and cultivate the four positive actions that will cause you to remember it. These are:

1. Intentionally lying to a guru or someone worthy of veneration in order to deceive them. It does not matter whether they are misled

or not or whether the words are many or few, so it is wrong to tell even small lies in jest.

2. Though you should regret the wrongs you have done, causing someone else to regret even slightly virtuous actions—which do not warrant regret—is a fault whether or not the other person regrets them. Instead, as much as you can encourage others to engage in whatever virtuous activities of the three vehicles—especially those of the Mahayana—that they are able. Inspire everone to aspire to supreme enlightenment.

3. Anyone who has merely recited the words of rousing bodhichitta is included among the ranks of the bodhisattvas, so it goes without saying that it is inappropriate to criticize them even the slightest bit. You must never disparage even ordinary beings but should praise them instead. Since all sentient beings have buddha nature, it is said that they are no different from buddhas in being worthy objects for us to purify our negative actions and gather the accumulations.

4. It is wrong to deceive, cheat, or trick others for even an ounce or a half cup with your body, speech, or mind in order to further your own aims. Instead, wishing to bring all sentient beings happiness and benefit in both this and their next lives, you must take others' benefit as your own responsibility. Even in conversation you should speak honestly, like parents and their children.

In short, it comes down to this: Give all profit and victory to others, and take all loss and defeat for yourself. Your intention alone is primary in the bodhisattva vow, so whatever your activity of body and speech, internally always strive to guard your mind. Train as extensively as you can in the cause of increasing bodhichitta, the two accumulations. *The Sutra Requested by Sagaramati* lists ten tasks of a bodhisattva:

[1.] Dwelling on the foundation of faith, serve a spiritual friend.

[2.] With intense diligence, seek the True Dharma everywhere.

[3.] With intense desire, never put aside striving at virtuous acts.

[4.] With carefulness, do not waste your actions.

[5.] Guide beings to spiritual maturity without attachment to your own virtue.

[6.] Uphold the True Dharma without regard for life or limb.

[7.] Do not be satisfied with the merit you have accumulated.

[8.] Assiduously gather the accumulation of wisdom.

[9.] Never be separate from the true meaning.

[10.] Through skill in means, seek whatever way is feasible.

Engage in these assiduously.

As for the precepts of engaged bodhichitta, if you want a good harvest, seeds alone are not enough—you have to put work into cultivating them. Likewise the mere intention to attain buddhahood is not enough. You must sow whatever practice of the conduct of enlightenment, great or small, that you can. This means the six transcendences: giving generously, guarding discipline, practicing patience, cultivating diligence, and training well in dhyana and prajna. As it is said:

> There is not anything at all
> In which the victors' children will not train.[27]

Therefore practice all the roots of virtue and rejoice in those that others do.

1. Loving-kindness is the wish that all sentient beings may encounter happiness they never had before and that they be brought to its cause, virtue. 2. Compassion is the wish that sentient beings may be free of their present suffering and that its cause, nonvirtue, be stopped. 3. Joy is rejoicing in the present physical comfort and mental happiness of others. 4. There is no difference in importance between you and any one sentient being such as your mother; you are equal. Equanimity is having no sense of closeness or distance toward that being or any sentient being and feeling the same for them—not being attached to one and averse to

another. Meditating in such a way for immeasurable sentient beings throughout the reaches of space without any distinction of enemy, friend, or neutral is called the four immeasurables. These are the quintessence of the Dharma and must be central to your practice from the time you begin the yoga of the Mahayana.

In the instructions of the Kadampa tradition, you develop lovingkindness in your being by contemplating the relationships of cause and effect: It is necessary to achieve buddhahood no matter what. As its cause, bodhichitta is necessary. The cause of that is compassion. The cause of compassion is loving-kindness. The cause of that is appreciating what others have done for you and feeling grateful. The cause of that is that you must know all sentient beings have been your parents. Once you know that, you must first contemplate the kindness of your loving mother and cultivate loving-kindness for her. Then, in the same vein, expand your meditation wider and wider to include all living, breathing creatures.

The two causes of ruin are pretending to be a bodhisattva from a hope to be seen by others as a good Dharma practitioner; or out of a wish for food, clothing, and reputation; or from a hope that things will go better for you than for others; and pretending to be other than you are and calling yourself a realized being or mahasiddha. Thus you must apply the remedy of meditating on the difficulty of obtaining a precious human rebirth and on impermanence.

Engaging in a few virtuous activities or a bit of Dharma practice while merely aspiring to enjoy the comforts of gods and humans in future lives is contrary to bodhichitta. As a remedy, you should remember the faults of samsara and karmic cause and effect. If you just think of your own aims and do not develop the wish to benefit others, you have made a fundamental mistake, so meditate on the equality of self and others as well as on exchanging yourself for others. This is especially important. You and all sentient beings are equal in wanting happiness. You are equal in not wanting to suffer. You are also equal in the dharmata, the lack of own being. You are one and they are many, so they are not just equal to you—they are far more important. Therefore you should wish to achieve buddhahood and then bring all sentient beings to that state. You must have a deep and certain conviction in your mind about this and not just leave it as a mere intellectual understanding.

To enhance this, do not cherish yourself but treasure any one sentient being far more than yourself, so that you would be willing to undergo even terrible suffering for the sake of others' happiness. Your actions and intentions must be solely for the benefit of others. Now, when we do even a trifling virtue, we do it to benefit ourselves. When we do what someone else tells us to do, we do it for that person's sake. Acting like this will not get us anywhere. Do everything you do—walking, pacing, lying down, and sitting,[28] not to mention Dharma activity—solely with the wish to benefit others.

When you are beset by illness and döns or pained by slander, when the afflictions increase and so forth, gather everything sentient beings do not want and heap it on top of that. When suffering occurs, know that it is karma from the past and do not be depressed; instead take on the suffering of others. When you are comfortable and happy, devote your wealth and influence towards virtuous ends. Do not wallow in sloth but employ your body and speech for virtue. Make aspiration prayers that all sentient beings be happy and comfortable. In brief, do not get entangled in self-interest no matter what you do, and make all your Dharma practice an antidote for ego-clinging.

Together with the breath you inhale, the blackness of all the suffering, wrongdoing, and obscurations of all sentient beings enters you through your nostrils and dissolves into your heart. When you breathe out, exhale through your nostrils all the virtue and happiness you have accumulated since beginningless time in the form of white light. Think that by giving each sentient being a portion, they all achieve buddhahood, and meditate on sympathetic joy. Continuously recite:

When happy, I dedicate my virtue to all—
May benefit and happiness fill space.
When sad, may the suffering of all ripen on me—
May the ocean of suffering run dry.

Even at the time of death, when you cannot practice anything else, do sending and taking once with your last breath.

When physical illness, mental suffering, lawsuits, debts, or anything unwanted occurs, do not resent others. Think that it is caused by your own self-cherishing and take the blame on yourself. Enemies, friends, and neutral people are the basis of mind-training and aids in purifying wrongdoing and obscurations, so think how very kind to you they all are.

Do not do or say anything with the hope that others will think you have no ego-clinging. Your behavior should be in accord with the vinaya—pure and sincere. Do not speak of others' faults. You should recognize that the faults you see in others are your own impure perceptions. Also give up pointing out others' flaws, speaking harshly, reciting wrathful mantras to nonhuman spirits, and so forth. Do not pass off onto others difficult tasks that fall upon you, burden others with blame for your own wrongs, or so forth. It is wrong to even think about delighting in an adversary's defeat, considering it good that an enemy has died, hoping for offerings and renown when another falls ill, and so forth.

Without regard for anything such as the state of your own health or what people might say about you, meditate on bodhichitta. Furthermore, meditate intently on those for whom it is hardest to generate compassion, such as adversaries and obstructive spirits. Abandon being sporadic in your Dharma practice due to a lack of certainty. Since practicing Dharma is for your own sake, do not boast about the hardships you are undergoing no matter how great they are. When others expose your faults, blame you, humiliate, beat or become irritated at you, do not respond—only meditate on compassion. Do not show your pleasure or displeasure over every little thing. If you cannot endure the slightest harm to yourself and do not do even the smallest thing to help others, you have missed the point of generating bodhichitta. Because exchanging yourself for others is an especially powerful type of skillful means, practice it with fortitude.

Merely developing bodhichitta purifies an immeasurable number of negative actions and causes virtuous actions to increase endlessly. The merit you accrue in one instant of bodhichitta is greater than the merit of offering to every buddha as many realms as there are grains of sand in the Ganges, each filled with precious jewels. Recounting bodhichitta's immeasurable benefits is unnecessary as it is the essence of all Dharma.

All the conduct of a bodhisattva such as the practice of the six transcendences arises from compassion alone. So do not just say, "I have been meditating for this many days or months," or look at one suffering being and say, "Poor thing! How sad!" Instead, train so that your compassion always extends to all sentient beings without bias or discrimination.

In order to ripen your own continuum, train in all aspects of virtuous activity. This is the discipline of gathering virtuous qualities. In order to ripen sentient beings, encourage them to practice the virtues that are appropriate for them. This is the discipline of benefiting beings. These two include all the vows of a bodhisattva, and failing to do either of the two when they could be done is a transgression for a bodhisattva, it is said. Therefore accomplish roots of virtue that are appropriate to the occasion and encourage others to do so as well. Feeling that just a bit is enough and clinging to indistinct experience that will not withstand adversity is nothing more than the fault of not having studied the Buddha's scriptures and the life stories of the great beings.

2. The Instructions on the Hundred-syllable Mantra that Purifies Misdeeds and Obscurations

There are two types of hundred-syllable mantras, the hundred-syllables of the Tathagata taught in *The Tantra of the Manifestation of the Three Samayas*[29] and the hundred-syllable mantra of Vajrasattva taught in many tantras. There are two kinds of hundred-syllable mantras of Vajrasattva, the peaceful hundred syllables of all families that can be changed into the name mantras of infinite supramundane deities, and the hundred syllables of the wrathful heruka taught in the *Highest Tantra of Speech*.[30] Although they may not all have exactly one hundred syllables, they are known as hundred-syllable mantras because they are all of the same mantra family.

Here I will describe the stages of visualization of the hundred syllables of the peaceful Vajrasattva. There are two traditions: that of a single figure in the form of a universal emperor according to the yoga tantra, and a coemergent one in union with consort according to the unexcelled tantra. Here, the custom is to meditate according to the yoga tantra tradition.

You are in your ordinary form. Above the crown of your head, the seed syllable PAM (ཪྃ), transforms into a lotus, and an A (ཨ) transforms into a moon seat. On top of that, a HŪM (ཧཱུྃ) becomes a white, five-pronged vajra marked with hūṃ at its center. Light rays radiating from the HŪM make offerings to the noble ones, benefit beings, and are reabsorbed, and it transforms into Vajrasattva, who is inseparable from your root guru. He is white with one face and two arms. His right hand holds a five-pronged vajra at his heart. His left holds a white silver bell at his hip. His right leg is extended and his left is bent in the posture of a sattva. He wears upper and lower garments of various silks and all the peaceful ornaments such as a jeweled diadem and so forth. His hair is bound in a topknot, and at the tip of that sits Guru Akshobhya, who represents his family. His body, adorned with the marks and signs and emitting immeasurable light rays, appears but lacks any nature, like a reflection of the moon in water. His three places are marked by the three seed syllables.[31] At his heart, on a lotus and moon seat, is a white HŪM (ཧཱུྃ) surrounded by the garland of the hundred-syllable mantra, white in color. The letters face outward, and beginning in the front, the mantra circles around clockwise like the coils of a snake. Light radiates out from the HŪM, inviting the buddhas and bodhisattvas of the ten directions and three times, who dissolve into the HŪM and mantra. Think that Vajrasattva becomes the combined essence of all the Jewels.

Supplicate him to purify your misdeeds and obscurations. Think that this causes wisdom nectar to flow from the seed syllable and mantra garland at his heart. It fills his entire body, and as if overflowing, descends in a white stream from the big toe of his right foot and enters you through the crown of your head. Like a river carrying away detritus, it flushes out through your orifices and pores all the misdeeds and obscurations you have accumulated from beginningless lifetimes (such as breakages and violations of samaya) in the form of soot and sludge; all illnesses in the form of pus, blood, and lymph; and all döns in the form of parasites and filth, along with your physical flesh and blood. These dissolve into the powerful golden earth. Your body is filled with pure wisdom nectar, and the excess overflows and touches Varajasattva's foot. Visualize this extremely clearly again and again.

As it is said:

If you are distracted by something else,
Reciting for aeons will bear no fruit.

Thus without even a moment's distraction, recite the hundred-syllable and six-syllable mantras at a moderate pace, clearly, correctly, and sonorously.

At the end, join your palms and recite the words of supplication and confession, "Protector, out of ignorant delusion..." Guru Vajrasattva is pleased, smiles, and reassures you saying, "Child of Noble Family, all of your misdeeds, obscurations, wrongs, and transgressions are purified from today onwards." He then melts into light and dissolves into you. Think that Vajrasattva's body, speech, and mind become inseparable from your own body, speech, and mind, and rest without reference point. If it is the end of the session, dedicate the merit.

The signs of having purified misdeeds are explained in the texts. Some particular ones include your body becoming light and needing little sleep, experiencing good health and a clear mind, having some minor experiences and realizations, and so forth.

As for the meaning of the practice: we must give up wrongdoing and accomplish virtue. Only the perfect Buddha knew correctly what to abandon and what to adopt and advised others about it. Believing his words and putting them into practice is internalizing their essential meaning.

Whether an action is virtuous or a misdeed, even if it is small at the time of the cause, its effect increases greatly at the time of the result. The results of misdeeds manifest as the lower realms, and the results of virtues as the higher realms. The actions you have done will not go to waste, and you will not experience karma you have not committed.

Actions that are motivated by desire, aversion, or ignorance but not actually physically or verbally expressed are mental actions. Those actually expressed are actions of body and speech. The mind must precede all actions, so it is said:

> Because it makes the world go dark,
> The mind is the root of poison.[32]

Misdeeds include the five heinous deeds, the five near heinous deeds, the ten nonvirtues, the four weighty actions, the eight perversions,[33] and so forth along with downfalls that are violations of the three types of vows, whether you have done them yourself, encouraged others to do them, or rejoiced at and praised them.

In brief, we carry the burden of a mountain of misdeeds and downfalls that we do not know about or feel but have accumulated in beginningless lifetimes. On top of that, almost all our present intentions and actions of body, speech, and mind just heap on additional misdeeds and obscurations due solely to the three poisons. Because of those wrongs, we are cursed and slandered by gods and humans in this life. Things often go wrong or don't work out. Our guardian deities forsake us, and döns and obstructive spirits take advantage of this. We are thrust into the ranks of the wretched. Our misdeeds cast a shadow on everything we are connected to, bringing bad luck. We have various bad dreams and are unhappy. Fatal accidents and severe, mortal illnesses occur. At the time of death, there is intense agony, fear, and suffering, and there is intense confusion in the bardo. And after death we will experience for a long time the agonizing suffering of the three lower realms in accord with the severity of our wrongdoing. Even if at some point we are born in the high realms, we will have short lives and ill health. Though you are innocent, enemies and lawsuits will appear, and there will be crop failures, epidemics, and war in your country. As the causally compatible result,[34] you will enjoy wickedness and your suffering will increase unceasingly.

It is not so that you must do wrongs that are unavoidable and will definitely benefit you, whether for the sake of subduing enemies and protecting friends; for the sake of wealth, possessions, or reputation; or for the sake of food, clothing and so forth. No matter how much you have, those will not benefit you even a sesame seed's worth at the time of death. Forget about reputation, possessions, children, spouses, and so forth—you will be powerless to take with you even a single morsel of food or a set of clothes. Alone you will wander to the lower realms. At that time there will be no one else with whom you can share the suffering that results from your misdeeds—you alone will experience it.

It is not hard for an enemy to change into a friend or a friend into an enemy, so daring to commit wrongs is to be caught by the maras and crazed by döns—it is great stupidity and ignorance. But up to now, we have not recalled even a single drawback and never said, "I can't let myself do this. I shall not." Think to yourself, "I could die at any time—will I even have time to purify my misdeeds? If I die without purifying any of them, what suffering will occur to me in the lower realms?" and so forth. Drive yourself to shame. You must meditate until you cannot sit still and are disconsolate.

Furthermore, if you hide your wrongs and keep them secret, they will grow more and more powerful—that is combining the seed of misdeeds with the water and fertilizer of deception. If you do not conceal your faults, but recognize them and admit them openly to others, they will not increase but will weaken instead. "The truth brings it to a close," it is said.

If in addition you apply yourself to the methods of purifying misdeeds with deep regret and confession, you will have no difficulty purifying misdeeds and downfalls completely. Furthermore, if embraced by skillful means, even a single virtue can overcome a great heap of wrongs.

To say, "I did this wrong" is to admit it. To have intense regret and mental anguish about it is confession. The meaning of confession is that you are disheartened and ashamed by the wrongs you have done and say from the depths of your heart with great admiration and respect to those who have not committed such wrongs, "Think of me with compassion—I pray that you purify this karma."

For this, the four powers must be fulfilled:

1. The power of remorse is to have such intense regret toward former misdeeds that you feel as sorry as if you had drunk poison.
2. The power of turning away from wrongs is to have a mind

that firmly resolves never to do that harmful action again,
even if your life is at stake.

3. The power of support is to go for refuge and generate
bodhichitta.

4. The power of applying the antidote is to accomplish whatever
virtue you can—such as the six methods of remedy and so
forth—with the intention of purifying misdeeds.

If you do not regret what you have done and just go through the
motions of confession, your misdeeds will not be purified. If you lack
the resolve to never do them again, all the confessions and virtues you
do will be pointless. A single confession by someone who has authenti-
cally taken refuge and developed bodhichitta has more power to purify
negative actions than one hundred thousand confessions by someone
who has neither taken refuge nor developed bodhichitta. One day of
confession by someone who has received empowerment purifies more
negative actions than years of confession by someone who has only
received the refuge and bodhisattva vows. This is because the powers of
support are progressively higher. Misdeeds and virtues are magnified in
the same way as well.

There are six methods of remedy:

1. Memorizing the names of the buddhas and bodhisattvas specifically praised for their ability to purify obscurations, such as
Amitabha, the Medicine Buddha, and Akshobhya, and reciting
them to others

2. Fashioning statues, texts, and stupas

3. Presenting offerings to those three representations, serving the
Sangha, offering mandalas and ganachakras if a vajrayana practitioner, and especially practicing the five methods of pleasing
the guru

4. Reciting the sutras and tantras taught by the Victor, such as the
Prajnaparamita sutras and *The Sutra of Great Liberation*

5. Reciting profound dharanis such as the hundred-syllable mantra of the Tathagata or the mantras of Sarvavid, Akshobhya, and so forth

6. Having confidence in buddha-nature and meditating on the meaning of selflessness: devote yourself to resting in a state free of focus on the three spheres—the misdeeds and obscurations to be purified; the deity and mantra that purify; and yourself, the person purifying—and meditate on either the actual profound yoga or the attitude compatible with it that all things are unreal, like an illusion.

Although any of these, if practiced effectively, is capable of completely purifying the causes and results of wrongdoing, the meditation and recitation of Vajrasattva is taught here in order to swiftly purify coarse misdeeds and obscurations that obstruct the arising of experience and realization in the main practice of mahamudra.

The misdeeds and obscurations we have accumulated in this life obscure experience the most because they are so recent. In particular, violations of the three types of vows, and especially, violations of the samaya of the guru's body, speech, and mind are extremely grave wrongs and downfalls. Violating other samayas of the secret mantra such as unethical use of the sangha's possessions and offerings to the gurus also obscures previous experiences and prevents new ones from arising. That is why the hundred-syllsable mantra of Vajrasattva is renowned as the best way to purify all of these.

Lord Atisha said, "Minor infractions and downfalls of the secret mantra vows constantly occur. For example, it is like cleaning a mandala plate and setting it down in an extremely dusty place—it is immediately covered in dust anew."

"Well then," someone asked, "Will there never be a time when the path arises in our beings?"

"But," he replied, "the secret mantra has many skillful methods, so just a single one can purify many subtle infractions and downfalls in an instant." He then gave them a long recitation practice of the hundred syllables.

Furthermore, the tantras of the ancient and new translation are unanimous in saying that it has immeasurable short-term and ultimate benefits. This point is encapsulated in one Indian text:

> Dharanis, mantras, mudras,
> Building stupas and mandalas
> Do not possess such merit
> As a single hundred syllables,
> The pervasive lord and five wisdoms in nature.
> The merit of someone who recites
> The hundred syllables properly
> Is ornamented by all the buddhas
> Who are as numerous as atoms.[35]

Furthermore:

> Those who know the hundred syllables
> Will not experience untimely death,
> Disease, or sorrow.

> Those who know the hundred syllables,
> Will not see poverty, suffering, or so forth.
> Their enemies will disappear,
> And all their wishes will be fulfilled.

> Knowing the hundred syllables,
> Those who want a son will have one,
> And those who want wealth will gain it.
> Those without a homeland will gain one.

Those who desire long life
Should memorize the hundred syllables.
Those whose life force is depleted
Will easily live three hundred years.
They will be happy in this life
And go to Sukhavati after death.

Those who know the hundred syllables
Cannot be harmed by dakinis,
Spirits, zombies, or the bhutas
Who cause fits or amnesia.

Even those who committed a great downfall,
Will definitely see the buddha.
By reciting the hundred syllables of secret mantra,
Fools will gain intelligence

And the unfortunate will gain fortune.
Disaster and suffering will be eradicated.
Even perpetrators of the five heinous deeds
Can be purified by reciting the hundred syllables.

In lifetime after lifetime,
They'll be born in emperors' families.
Eventually they'll be liberated
And achieve buddhahood itself.

It is said that if you exert yourself at this, minor and moderate transgressions will be fully purified. Even major ones will not increase; they will be suppressed and gradually purified.

Generally, if you develop a belief in karma and result, it will be impossible not to feel remorse for wrongdoing, and then your confession will be authentic. That will purify your being, and there will be no way not to develop experience and realization. But we just follow the customs of the monastery and race through the recitation out of obligation without genuine belief or regret. The fact that experience and realization vie with turtle fur for rarity seems to come down to this.

3. The Instructions for Mandala Offerings, Which Perfect the Two Accumulations

There is nothing wrong with a small mandala plate if it is made of good material. A mandala of poor material such as clay or wood, ought to be large. If you lack resources, it is permissible to use a board, piece of slate, and so forth or to visualize one if you cannot afford even that. The most important thing is the visualization.

You will need two mandala plates. Use the one that is larger and of better material as the mandala of accomplishment and the other as the offering mandala. For the offering piles, precious substances such as gold, silver, and so forth are best. Conch and cowry are next best. The least is clean grain such as barley or rice moistened and tinted with saffron water. If you can afford it, use new ones each time. If not, replenish the grains with fresh ones that you have set aside. The grains you offer should not be used for your own consumption later but should be offered to the Three Jewels

Wipe the mandala of accomplishment three times while visualizing. Cleanse it with OṂ AMṚITA...[36] and purify it with SVABHĀVA ...[37] From the state of emptiness, meditate that the mandala itself is a jeweled palace with all the characteristics, in the middle of which the five piles are the sources of refuge, as in refuge practice. It is not necessary to visualize the lake and wish-fulfilling tree. Meditate that the Dharma protectors are in the spaces in between. Lights radiating from the three seed syllables in their three places invite innumerable wisdom deities from their natural abodes, who dissolve inseparably into them. Place it on a high, covered shelf before you and supplicate them to remain. If possible, surround it with the five types of offerings.[38] If you cannot afford a mandala of accomplishment or if you are doing it as a continuing practice,[39] visualize the recipients of your offerings in the sky in front of you.

Next, take the offering mandala in your left hand and hold some flower petals in your right fist. While reciting the hundred-syllable mantra, polish the surface of the mandala plate with your right wrist three times clockwise. Meditate that whatever illnesses, döns, misdeeds, obscurations, and filth of yourself and others—the environment and all beings—subsumed within perceiver and perceived are all thoroughly cleansed and purified. Because the mandala represents the stainless nature of mind, you should polish it so well that there is not even the slightest haze or smudge on it. In general, offering mandalas is about interdependent connections, so use the finest and most valuable materials you can and observe cleanliness while practicing—do not just do it any old way.

For the actual visualization, the presentations of the world taught in the Kalachakra and in the abhidharma are different. Since mahamudra is the ultimate essence of all the classes of tantra, it makes no difference which of the two you visualize in the preliminary practices. But here the custom is to use the abhidharma version as it is more well known.

While saying "OM VAJRA BHŪMI…" and so forth, if you have some, sprinkle saffron water on the mandala to symbolize anointing it with the moisture of bodhichitta. Meditate that the mandala becomes a vast and spacious golden ground as even as the palm of a hand. On top of that gathers an ocean whose fragrant waters have the eight qualities. If scented water is not available, scatter the mandala with flower petals. It is not necessary to visualize the foundation below of mandalas of wind, fire and water. While saying "OM VAJRA REKHE…," sprinkle grains counterclockwise around the rim in the manner of the iron mountains, and at the same time meditate that the ring of the Horse Face mountains made of flaming iron is created.

There are those who at this point say HŪM and place a drop of scented water or a pile of flowers in the center, but in this tradition there is no such custom. Likewise one could visualize Mount Meru and so forth arising from their respective seed syllables, but here we meditate on them as being complete the moment they are thought of.

Next, recite the words of the text while at the same time visualizing their meaning in order. In the middle of the ocean is Mount Meru. It has four sides and four terraces and grows wider at the top. Its eastern slope is made of crystal, its southern of vaidurya,[40] its western of ruby, and its northern of emerald. The oceans, sky, and continents in each direction appear in the color of each side.

Surrounding it are the seven square, golden mountain ranges: Yoke Holder, Plow Holder, Acacia Tree, Lovely to Behold, Horse's Ear, Bowing Down, and Rim Holder, each of which is half the height of the previous. In between and surrounding them are the seven Playful Seas filled with waters that have the eight qualities and with the various treasures of the nagas—wish-fulfilling jewels and so forth. Beyond that are the continents: In the east is the white, semi-circular continent of Superior Body; in the south is the blue, trapezoidal Rose Apple Land; in the west is the red, round Bountiful Cow; and in the north is the green, square Unpleasant Sound. On either side of each continent is a satellite continent, the same shape and color as the main one.

Within those lands, on top of Mount Meru, and in the sky above are a mountain of diamonds, vaidurya, sapphires, emeralds, pearls, gold, silver, crystals and other jewels; a grove of wish-fulfilling trees that rain down whatever is wanted and needed; a herd of wish-fulfilling cows from whose every hair springs whatever is desired; and inexhaustible untilled crops that dispel all hunger. There are the seven articles of royalty: a thousand-spoked wheel made from gold found in the river Jambu; an eight-faceted gem which is bright as the sun and which rains down what is wanted and needed for many leagues; a queen lovely to behold who possesses the thirty two qualities of feminine perfection; a most handsome and intelligent minister who can see underground treasures; a white elephant with seven sturdy limbs, draped with a golden net, who moves unhindered through the sky; an excellent horse whose coat is the color of a peacock's neck and who can circle the four continents in one morning; and a general who has mastered the sixty-four athletic skills.

There are also a vase of great treasure that grants an endless supply of the seven types of jewels—sapphire and the others; the white goddess of charm with vajra fists resting on her hips; the yellow goddess of garlands holding strings of jewels and garlands of flowers; the red and white goddess of music holding a lute; the green goddess of dance who is dancing; the yellow goddess of flowers holding a bouquet of flowers; the blue goddess of incense holding a censer; the pink goddess of lamps holding a lamp; and the green goddess of perfume holding a conch shell full of fragrant perfume. In the northeastern sky is the sun, a blazing orb of fire crystal, and in the southwestern sky is the moon, an orb of water crystal with cooling powers. Many constellations of stars and planets shine their light.

On top of Mount Meru is the palace Utterly Conquering in the center and Vishnu's city Lovely to Behold. On the four sides are the four parks Colorful Chariots and so forth. There are the trees Earth Piercing All-Gathering[41] and so forth, flat rocks such as *armonik*,[42] and the gathering place of the gods Good Dharma. In the sky above that in ascending order are Conflict Free, Joyous, and so forth—the abodes of the gods supported on clouds of jewels—as well as an immeasurable array of wealth.

Above, below, and in between all of these are the eight auspicious symbols—the precious parasol, the golden fish, the vase, the lotus, the white conch swirling to the right, the endless knot, the victory banner, and the wheel; the eight auspicious substances—a mirror, vermilion, white conch, *durva* grass, *bilva*,[43] yogurt, and mustard seeds; the seven semi-precious articles—the jeweled bed, throne, cushion, sword, boots, snakeskin, and robe; many types of medicine that cure illness such as the six good medicines; vital essences and substances of accomplishment; various substances that prolong life such as strong elixirs and the good vase; objects that bring intelligence and renown—swords, books, lutes, other musical instruments, and so forth; wondrous offerings such as a shower of rainbow-colored flowers, ponds of perfumed water, lotus gardens, and magical birds and animals; as well as many attending gods and goddesses. It is, in brief, filled to overflowing with all the abundance of gods and humans, none left out. Mentally take anything in the ten directions that is unowned and can be given, and offer it.

A billion such worlds with the four continents, Mount Meru, and so forth is called a World of the Great Three Thousands. Offer to the guru and the Three Jewels uncountable such universes all filled with Samantabhadra's clouds of offerings as well as your own and all other beings' bodies, possessions, parents, relatives, and roots of virtue. Make aspiration prayers that we not encounter obstacles on the path to enlightenment, and that we attain the supreme siddhi of mahamudra in this very lifetime. Your hands never empty of offerings, visualize offering and mentally make aspirations again and again without interruption.

When accumulating repetitions, if your mind cannot cope with so many things to visualize, definitely visualize the ground, iron mountains, Mount Meru, the four continents, and the sun and moon, and then just imagine that this realm and everywhere there is space are filled with offerings and that you are presenting them.

Longer and shorter mandala offerings range from five to thirty-seven features, but here it is the thirty-seven feature mandala. The manner of placing the heaps should be learned through a visual transmission. When accumulating mandalas, just offer the seven-feature one.

At the end, meditate that light radiates from the recipients of the offerings you have been visualizing on the mandala of accomplishment and strikes you and all sentient beings, completely perfecting the two accumulations. Think that the deities melt into light and dissolve into you. Dedicate the merit.

The manner in which actual signs of perfecting the two accumulations appear as experiences or in dreams is explained in texts. But in particular, the truest signs are your mind turning strongly towards Dharma and your actions that are in harmony with the Dharma being accomplished without effort.

To elaborate a bit, if you develop authentic mahamudra meditation, all accumulations of merit and purification of obscurations are contained within that. However those who have not previously gathered the accumulations will not develop authentic meditation. There are very few people who have accumulated merit or have good karmic propensities. Though it is a given that all who enter the gate of the Dharma and gain faith have a few virtuous imprints in their being, those cannot be awakened immediately, just as it is difficult for there to be a blaze without the condition of a tiny spark. Until the roots of virtue have been awakened, experience and realization will not arise. Even if a little arises, it will not develop and increase. Thus producing anew superior roots of virtue acts as the condition for awakening the imprints from the past and will ripen your being swiftly, making great experience arise.

As far as the accumulations to gather, the commentaries by bodhisattvas[44] say there are three accumulations: generosity, means, and aspirations are the accumulation of merit; discipline, patience, and diligence are the accumulation of discipline; and dhyana, prajna, power, and wisdom are the accumulation of wisdom. The sutras teach two accumulations: generosity and discipline comprise the accumulation of merit. Prajna comprises the accumulation of wisdom. Patience, diligence, and dhyana are included in both. If these are not embraced by bodhichitta, they are karmas that are precursors to merit, so they will not become causes that liberate you from the higher realms. If embraced by bodhichitta, they are karmas that are precursors to liberation and become causes of buddhahood. If in addition they are embraced by the view that is purified of the three spheres, they are the undefiled accumulations and thus the actual method for achieving enlightenment.

There are three types of generosity:

1. Material generosity is giving away food, clothing, necessities—even ink and paper—whatever you are able, whatever you can afford. At the very least, do not leave the beggar with an empty stomach. Think that in the future when you have the dominion and so forth of a universal emperor, you will give away your body and all your possessions.

2. Giving freedom from fear is giving medicine to the sick; protecting others from demons; showing the path along precipices; escorting beings through dangerous places; preventing obstacles to others' practice and discipline; and protecting others from punishment, enemies, thieves, wild animals, natural disasters, and so forth. You should actually practice this as much as you can. Pray to be able in the future to protect beings from all suffering of the lower realms on up.

3. Giving Dharma is explaining—if you are capable of doing so—as much Dharma to others as you can without pride or regard for reputation, in such a way as will definitely benefit them, temporarily and ultimately. If you are not capable of this, imagine you are teaching humans and nonhumans the Dharma and read aloud sutras and dharanis spoken by the Buddha.

There are three types of discipline:

1. The discipline of refraining from bad behavior is guarding against all naturally unwholesome acts such as the ten nonvirtues and all disobedient unwholesome acts such as infringing the precepts of the three types of vows as if protecting your life.[45]

2. The discipline of gathering virtuous qualities is not limiting yourself to just one kind of virtue—put into practice in every way all those that you are able to do and pray to be able to accomplish those that you cannot.

3. The discipline of benefitting beings is doing whatever you are

able from the time you develop bodhichitta onward to benefit others. Make vast aspirations to accomplish those you are unable to do—it is not enough merely for your own being to be uncontaminated by wrongs and downfalls.

There are also three types of patience:

1. The patience of paying no heed to harm is paying no heed to verbal abuse, beatings, blows, seizure of property, violent robbery, and so forth from others.
2. The patience of accepting suffering is disregarding a lack of necessary conditions, illness, hunger, thirst, fatigue, or exhaustion when practicing Dharma.
3. The patience of forbearing the recognition of the Dharma is the ability of the mind to comprehend without fear the profound skillful means of mantra, the vast deeds of the buddhas and bodhisattvas, the meaning of emptiness beyond elaborations, and so forth.

There are three types of diligence:

1. Armor-like diligence is the dauntless enthusiasm for virtue that neither ignores minor virtues thinking, "It is alright not to do that," nor gets discouraged about major ones thinking, "I can't do that much."
2. The diligence of application is when you are engaging in virtue, not being lazy until that virtue has been completed.
3. Irreversible diligence is not getting frustrated once you have embarked on something, even when the benefits and signs of progress do not immediately arise, but instead, increasing your endurance until you achieve its result.

There are three types of dhyana:

1. The dhyana of resting comfortably in the visible[46] is workability of body and mind.
2. The dhyana of achieving qualities is the clairvoyances, miraculous powers, and so forth.
3. The dhyana that benefits beings is to benefit them through the power of samadhi and so forth.

For these three to arise, you must develop faultless calm abiding meditation. Since calm abiding is the foundation of all qualities, establishing a solid basis in it is indispensable. For this to occur, mental solitude is necessary. This comes from physical isolation. This results from having few aims and few activities. As the cause of this, you must have few desires. That means being content with only meager food, clothing, and shelter. In brief, the source of calm abiding is to have few desires and be content.

For prajna:

1. The prajna that knows the ultimate truth due to realizing the way things are, emptiness
2. The prajna that knows relative truth—the definite recognition of cause, result, and interdependence
3. The prajna that knows how to benefit beings—knowing the four means of nurturing disciples

Alternately, there are the three prajnas of listening, contemplating, and meditating. Practice these as much as you can.

By gathering the accumulations in this way, in the short term you gain the immeasurable rewards and well-being of gods and humans. Ultimately, once you have perfected the two accumulations and the six transcendences, you will become an omniscient buddha.

You need not think that you lack the materials and facilities to gather the accumulations. It is said that having some faith and prajna within yourself is an inconceivable method for accumulating merit. When motivated by bodhichitta, even if you only offer the seven branches, all obscurations will be exhausted and the two accumulations will become equal to the extent of space.

Furthermore, prostrations alone are said to have ten benefits:

A good complexion, beauty, venerable speech,
Influence over associates, affection of gods and humans,
The company of the holy, great dignity,
Prosperity, higher realms, and liberation.

It is said that by making a single prostration with great respect, you will attain the power of a universal emperor as many times as the number of atoms in the great powerful golden earth underneath your five extended limbs. Even simply joining your palms in prayer to the Three Jewels brings ten benefits such as having a pleasing form, a large retinue, and so forth. The sutras distinctly describe a great many such benefits.

All the early masters of Atisha's Kadampa tradition concentrated day and night on the seven-branch offering alone and nothing else. All the previous Kagyu masters extending back to the peerless Gampopa also had this custom, but these days, when it is as if the teachings are gradually declining, we have no interest at all in the need to perfect the accumulations. Even if we have a little, our faith and diligence are both so weak that we do not put gathering the accumulations into practice. The few representations of the Buddha's body, speech, and mind we have are covered with dust. Those who are more audacious stuff them under tattered hats and clothing. One person in a hundred has offering bowls and an altar, but leaves them to collect dust. We needlessly primp and preen ourselves but have never even offered a single flower to the Three Jewels while motivated by emptiness and compassion. Without ever having recited the seven-branch offering, we say, "I have no merit," but where does merit come from? The cause of merit is gathering the accumulations, the Buddha said.

Even if it is just one grain of barley, we eat it ourselves if it is edible and offer it if it is not. Though we are not deprived of gold, silver, fine silk, horses, cattle, and other wealth, we say:

I have no merit and am destitute;
I have no other wealth at all to offer.[47]

Then we proudly fill a small lamp and offer a *shalse* the size of a finger. Will any merit come to all those who lie to the Three Jewels? Therefore it is extremely important to gather accumulations commensurate to your wealth.

It is said in the sutras and tantras that there is no more profound way to gather the accumulations than the seven branches. Of these, the latter are more meritorious than the earlier—offering is more meritorious than prostration, confessing misdeeds more so than that, rejoicing still more so, and so forth. Recite either long or short versions as you wish. Thinking about the meaning is the crucial point. Merely mouthing the words is deceiving yourself.

In terms of offerings, there is none you can proffer with extended arms that is more meritorious than a mandala. It also fulfills aspects of the six transcendences, so the benefits of all of them come automatically. The immeasurable benefits of offering the mandala are explained elsewhere. *The Sutra of Building a House* says that by merely offering the mandala, you will become a lord of the gods' realms and the four continents. Implicitly, this teaches that by merely anointing the mandala with saffron water and placing a flower on it, you will be reborn as a god in the realm of the Four Great Kings. This, in brief, is the reason why the instructions on mandala offerings, which are extremely profound means to swiftly perfect the accumulations, are taught as a preliminary.

Though all those who imagine themselves to be generous may give offerings numbering in the hundreds, thousands, ten thousands, hundred thousands, and so forth, it is impossible for them to give more. Such offerings are inevitably contaminated by self-centered thoughts of

"I gave that much," as well as by hopes for fame, recognition, and so forth. There is also the hope and anxiety of wondering whether the guru will accept them. And no matter how many the recipients of the offerings, they are not more than a hundred or a thousand.

But mandala offerings are vast since they include the universe, sentient beings, and the wealth that fills all of space. They have no stains such as the pride of thinking, "I am someone who offers mentally-emanated offerings!" There is also no hope or anxiety as to whether the Three Jewels will accept them or not. Because you visualize the Jewels of the ten directions and four times, the recipients of your offerings are excellent and vast. Thus in all respects there is no way you will not perfect the accumulations through them, so do them assiduously.

In addition, construct new temples and representations of the body, speech, and mind, and restore old ones. Respectfully serve the Sangha. If you have no resources, sweep temples, prostrate, and circumambulate. Recite praises and supplications. Even as much as raising one palm in prayer or tossing a single flower into the air while visualizing the Buddha is said to be immeasurably meritorious.

We are not beasts who do not know good from evil, nor have we assumed wretched forms in which we would be unable to recite even a single MAṆI even if we knew we should. At this time, we have a precious human body and do not lack the chance to practice Dharma. Do not let this human life go to waste—it is crucial to plant a few virtuous imprints in our beings no matter what.

4. Guru Yoga, Which Brings Blessings Swiftly

Purify into emptiness with the SVABHĀVA mantra. From the nature of emptiness there are a lotus, corpse, and sun as a seat, on top of which you are Vajra Varahi, visualized in the general manner. When you meditate on your body in its ordinary form, the impure cannot receive blessings. Visualizing yourself as the yidam creates the interdependent connections so that the blessings may be received easily and rapidly.

Although you could meditate on any yidam that appeals to you, Vajra Varahi herself is the mother who gives birth to all the buddhas. She is in essence mahamudra, appearing in the form of the coemergent mother. Because this type of yogini is dear to us, the blessings are swift. She is also the secret yidam of Marpa, Milarepa, and Gampopa. Due to these interdependent connections, here the custom is to visualize her.

Imagine that either above your head or in the sky in front of you is a jeweled throne supported by eight snow-lions and covered with fine, divine fabrics. On top of it on a lotus-moon seat is the combined essence of all the Buddhas of the three times, your root guru in the form of Vajradhara, as in the practice of going for refuge. In a column above him are the Kagyu masters up through Vajradhara, surrounded by an ocean of the siddhas of the practice lineages such as the Drikung, Drukpa, Tsalpa, Taklung, and so forth. Additionally, the gurus of lineages of the Great Perfection, the Six Yogas, Path and Result, Pacification Chöd, and Mind Training gather like clouds. Surrounding them are the gatherings of yidams, buddhas, bodhisattvas, heroes, dakinis, dharma protectors, and guardians. They have been wholly established from the very beginning, present as the inseparable samaya and wisdom beings.

With devotion that is not mere words, with the strength of dedication from the depths of your heart and a cry of longing pray, "Pervasive lord, whose nature is of all things..." and so forth. Offer the seven branches and aspirations by reciting the prayer beginning, "In the dharma expanse palace of Akanishtha..." and recite long or short supplications such as the mahamudra lineage prayer as appropriate. Then, without allowing your mind to be distracted by anything else, recite and accumulate the four-line prayer "My mothers throughout space..." and in particular the six-line supplication that is the vajra words of Lord Dusum Khyenpa.

At the end, supplicate the glorious gurus and others to grant you empowerment. Due to this, the surrounding retinue melts into light and dissolves into the lineage gurus. The lineage gurus then melt one into another. They melt into light and dissolve into your root guru, who becomes the essence of all Three Jewels combined.

White light radiates from his forehead and dissolves into the space between your eyebrows. This purifies obscurations of body such as killing. You receive the vase empowerment and are empowered to meditate on the creation phase during the time of the path. You become a fortunate one who will achieve the nirmanakaya as a result.

In a similar fashion, red light radiates from the guru's throat and dissolves into your throat, purifying your obscurations of speech such as lying. You receive the secret empowerment and are empowered to mediate on channels and winds. You become a fortunate one who will achieve the sambhogakaya.

Blue light radiates from the guru's heart and dissolves into your heart, purifying mental obscurations such as wrong views. You receive the prajna-wisdom empowerment and are empowered to meditate on absorption. You become a fortunate one who will attain the dharmakaya.

White, red, and blue lights radiate from the guru's three places and dissolve into your forehead, throat, and heart. This purifies the obscurations that are equally of body, speech, and mind contained within the afflictive and cognitive obscurations as well as the obscurations to absorption.[48] You receive the fourth empowerment and are empowered to meditate on mahamudra, inseparable awareness and emptiness. You become a fortunate one who will attain the essence kaya.

Once again, in response to your fervent devotion, the guru—with a pleased, radiant smile—melts into a globe of light that enters you through the crown of your head and dissolves into your heart. Imagine that the guru's mind and your mind become inseparable, and then let your mind be and rest evenly as long as you can in the uncontrived, uncontaminated nature uninterrupted by thought.

When you arise from that, think that whatever appearances arise are the various manifestations of the guru's body. All sounds are their speech, the empty yet audible natural sound of the channels. Whatever movement and thoughts arise in the mind are the spontaneous energy of the vajra-wisdom. Then dedicate the merit.

Between meditation sessions, when you are walking, think that you are circumambulating the guru, who is seated on a lotus-moon seat in the sky to your right. When eating or drinking, imagine that your food and drink melt into nectar that you offer to your guru, who is is seated on a red lotus in your throat. Meditate that everything you say is a supplication and that all movement, sitting, and activities are service to the guru. When going to sleep, meditate that the guru, an inch in size, sits in the center of your heart, and that his light illuminates your body and room. Fall asleep in that state. As soon as you wake up, imagine the guru sitting on the crown of your head and pray to him with faith and dedication. Also meditate in this way whenever you are sitting. When you get a new house, clothes, or so forth, offer the best of these to the guru, actually or mentally.

When ill, imagine the guru an inch in size at the location of the illness. Think that nectar drips from him, cleansing and purifying all sickness. Imagine that illness, misdeeds, and obscurations are methods of purification that come from the guru's blessings, and meditate on joy. If demonic displays arise, think that these are the play of the guru's activity, urging you to practice virtue.

In brief, meditate that any happiness that occurs is the guru's blessing and any suffering that occurs is also the guru's compassion. Use these as supports to increase your devotion and do not look elsewhere for ways to remedy them or to rid yourself of them. This is a crucial point.

There are some points to be understood here: Whatever instruction you meditate on—be it of the secret mantra vajrayana in general or the completion phase in particular—you must make the guru's blessings the path. The authentic path will not arise in your being until you have received the blessings. It is said that if students with samaya have heartfelt devotion for an authentic vajra master, they will achieve the supreme and ordinary siddhis even without any other methods. Once you lack devotion for your guru, though, you might finish all the approaches and accomplishments of the yidams of the four classes of tantras, but you will never attain supreme siddhi. You will also have to lower your expectations for many of the ordinary siddhis such as long life, attracting wealth, and charisma. Some of them you will not accomplish, and others you might accomplish to some degree but only with great difficulty, so that path is not profound. But if unmistaken devotion does arise in your being, it will dispel obstacles to the path, enhance your practice, and accomplish all supreme and ordinary siddhis without depending on anything else. This is the reason why this practice is called "the profound path of guru yoga."

For both master and disciple, lacking compassion, being quick to anger, being hateful, holding grudges, being inflated with pride or strongly attached to wealth and family, lacking in verbal and physical self-control, and praising themselves are great faults that must be given up.

In particular, there are masters who teach and explain the practices of the channels, winds, mudras, mantras, the collections of activity, or the essential points of the profound perfection stage to crowds of ordinary people. They claim to possess oral instructions others lack and then reveal the profound view and conduct of secret mantra to the public. Their conduct is polluted. They prattle on about high views. They crave the wealth and belongings of the Three Jewels intensely. They are deceitful and totally immoral, giving empowerments and instructions without a lineage and reveling in the pleasures of alcohol and sex. Not knowing how to teach the unmistaken path, they fabricate teachings that contradict the Dharma. Such masters have been blessed by demons, so you must avoid them at all costs.

A master should not make a profound connection in the beginning with students who lack faith, do not keep samaya, flatter new acquaintances, have too many ideas, and so forth unless it seems possible to gradually improve their minds.

The characteristics of a guru are explained at length in all the sutras and tantras. At the very least, their faith and samaya should be unimpaired; they should have completed the approach and accomplishment practices and know the rituals; they should not cling strongly to the eight worldly concerns; and they should have practiced to some degree the Dharma they explain to others. At the very least, students should have stable faith, be able to maintain samaya, and not associate with negative companions.

The examination of the characteristics of master and student should precede empowerments or Dharma teachings. Once a connection has been made through an empowerment or Dharma teaching, even if the guru has committed all four defeats, they are solely worthy of devotion—it is wrong to lose faith, criticize, scrutinize them, and so forth. As it is said:

> If you hear but a single verse
> Yet don't consider him a guru,
> Reborn a dog a hundred times,
> You'll then be born untouchable.

In these times you will not find a guru who has abandoned all faults and perfected all qualities. Were even it possible to find one or two, with our impure perception we would see their good qualities as faults, as has happened many times such as when Devadatta saw faults in the Bhagavan Buddha. These days, most people are only predisposed to accumulate negative karma, so they see faults as qualities and qualities as faults. Or they see those who inwardly lack even a single one of the Dharmic qualities that they exhibit outwardly as being holy. Thus it is hard to even know how to examine anyone. Especially in teaching the path of mahamudra, just as the designs on a mold are reproduced on the clay, the disciple cannot develop ultimate realization in their being without a guru who has realization.

Therefore once you receive a transmission passed down from peerless Gampopa, Dusum Khyenpa, Shang Tsalpa, Götsangpa, and so forth, if you take the one for whom you have the greatest faith as your root guru and supplicate them, they have promised you will receive their blessings. In particular, the Buddha prophesied that the peerless Gampopa would propagate the teachings of mahamudra, so all those who have longing for mahamudra should place their trust in Lord Gampopa. This is a crucial point. You should also meditate on your root guru as inseparable from him.

Once you have received the lineage of blessings from someone such as the Karmapa or his heart sons, considering him your root guru is sufficient on its own; further examination is unnecessary. It is not necessary to place your hopes on any other oral lineage—all those who have preceded the guru were great beings who have been prophesied and who passed down realization—the ultimate wisdom—from one to the next, so he is definitely able to bless others' mind streams.

Even if you are not able to hear the Dharma from a famous guru such as a lineage holder, if you take another guru who has experience and realization as your root guru, you will receive the blessings. Whether the guru is actually an ordinary being or an emanation of a buddha or bodhisattva, if you pray to him while meditating that he is a buddha, all the buddhas, bodhisattvas, and yidam deities will enter the body, speech and mind of that vajra master and work for the benefit of beings. From *The Mukhagama of Manjushri*:

> Any sentient being who belittles
> A vajra bearer of the future
> Belittles me, so therefore I
> Abandon them all for a time.

And:

> I dwell in his body and receive
> The offerings of other practitioners.
> Those who please him will purify
> The karmic obscurations in their own being.

Thus pleasing your guru pleases all the buddhas. If you commit a wrong against him, it is no different from committing a wrong against all the buddhas. Also if you offer to him, you gain the same merit as from offering to all the buddhas, and your obscurations will be extinguished. Innumerable sutras and treatises say that our attainment of supreme siddhi depends solely on the guru and that immeasurable benefits accrue through our devotion and offerings to him. It says in the tantras:

> Meditating on a hundred thousand deities' bodies
> Is not even worth a hundred thousandth part
> Of focusing undistracted on the guru's body.
> Reciting the approach and accomplishment
> A hundred trillion times has not even a hundred thousandth
> Of the power of supplicating the guru thrice.
> Meditating on the completion phase for aeons
> Is not even a twenty-thousandth part
> Of the guru merely appearing in your mind.

From *The Clear Lamp*:

> Child of noble family, greater than the mass of all the bhagavan
> buddhas who dwell in the ten directions and the merit born
> from the vajra body, speech, and mind of those bhagavan bud-
> dhas is the merit of a single pore of the master. If you ask why
> this is so, child of noble family, bodhichitta is the essence of the
> buddhas' wisdom.[49]

Generally speaking there is no difference at all between a guru with
whom you study the sutras of the Mahayana and Foundation Vehicles
and a guru from whom you receive the transmissions and instructions
of the secret mantra other than a slight difference in their significance.

When we talk about gurus against whom you can commit the first
root downfall[50] and break samaya, this depends upon yourself, so such
gurus are not necessarily identified as your root guru alone. Once you
have received a tantric empowerment, you must guard against the first
root downfall for all the gurus with whom you have Dharma connections. Thus no matter how much or little Dharma from the sutras or the
tantras you may have received, from then on it is important to not accumulate any misdeeds. If you have no Dharma connection to them, the
lineage gurus may not be your own gurus and thus you may not be able
to commit a downfall with regard to them. Even so, it is never right to
belittle or criticize them or so forth.

Generally do not examine sentient beings' faults. Know them to be
your mothers, be grateful, and meditate on loving-kindness and compassion. In particular, do not analyze the faults of anyone who has started to practice Dharma. Knowing that we are like people in the same
boat, think only of their positive qualities, rejoice, and have devotion.
Especially do not examine the guru's faults. It says in *The Noble Sutra of
the Mudra Engaging in Producing the Power of Faith*:

> Criticizing a single bodhisattva has greater negative conse-
> quences than stealing the possessions of all the sentient beings

in the billionfold universe and destroying all the stupas. Those who, due to whatever circumstance, develop contempt for and revile a bodhisattva will be born in the Wailing Hell with a body five hundred leagues in size and five hundred heads, mouths, and tongues, and each of their tongues will be plowed by five hundred plows.

Thus insulting holy beings is an incalculably great offense. Insulting bodhisattvas in particular and yogis of the secret mantra especially is far graver.

Furthermore, we do not know who may be a holy person or who may be practicing yoga internally. It is said that other than a perfect buddha, no individual is able to truly measure another. Thus speaking badly of and criticizing anyone else sweeps away your own positive qualities. Examining faults in others is self-destructive by nature, so it is important to post a watchman to examine solely your own faults.

We can see now that many undesired things befall everyone who lacks faith in the guru and perceives Dharma practitioners impurely. Others see them as adversaries. They die in unpleasant ways amid ill omens. They are the target of everyone's criticism. But all those who respectfully serve a guru and perceive others purely are naturally happy and have good reputations. Everyone praises, respects, and reveres them, and they die in pleasant circumstances amid excellent omens. These things we can see and hear for ourselves.

In the words of the Kagyu forefathers:

If you see the guru as a buddha, you will receive a buddha's blessing. If you see him as a bodhisattva, you will receive a bodhisattva's blessing. If you see him as a siddha, you will receive a siddha's blessing. If you see him as an ordinary person—a good spiritual friend—you will receive the corresponding blessings. If you have no devotion for him, you will receive no blessing whatsoever.

1. Thus there is no other buddha to be found elsewhere who is superior to your root guru—he is the combined essence of all the Jewels throughout the ten directions and three times. The positive qualities of the Jewels are limitless, and all of them are the manifestation of this root guru. Not only that, all the individuals everywhere who are now working for the benefit of beings, the sun and moon, herbal medicines, and even boats and bridges are the guru's display. Consider anyone who has given you an empowerment, transmission, or instruction—even those who taught you to read and write—to be an expression of your root guru. In short, resolve that he is a buddha.

2. No matter how amazing the buddhas, yidams, and Kagyu forefathers are, you have not seen their faces. You have not heard their speech. Even if you were to meet them, they could do nothing greater than what your guru does. Though there have been countless buddhas in the past, and infinite buddhas, bodhisattvas, gurus, and yidams now dwell in the ten directions, you have not had the fortune to meet a single one of them, even in a dream. But this root guru is teaching you the complete and unmistaken methods for attaining buddhahood in one lifetime and one body. Even if you ground your whole body into dust, you could not repay his kindness.

3. It should not be that you think about your guru when he pays attention to you—giving you teachings, gifts, and so forth—but forget about him when far away. You should not remember him when illness or misfortune occurs but not when you are well. Whether you are walking, pacing, lying down, or sitting, whether you are happy or sad—at all times, no matter what occurs—think of nothing but the guru.

4. It should not be that you occasionally think of your guru and say, "I go for refuge," or that you consider it amazing to recite a few supplications. Moved to tears and your hairs standing on end, your longing should be so fervent that it is able to suddenly cast awareness aside, stop ordinary appearances, and produce an unidentifiable experience.

When these four are present, that is the authentic devotion that makes you able to receive blessings and suddenly develop realization. The key to the rapid receipt of blessings is to meditate on the guru as a buddha.

Furthermore, if you are practicing mahamudra, you should think of the guru as the naked dharmakaya. If you want to extend your life, think of him as Amitayus or White Tara. If you want to cure illness, think of him as the Medicine Buddha. For döns, think of him as their remedy. You must view him as inseparable from the principal deities of any of the mandalas from the tantras. This is the meaning of calling him "the Guardian of the Mandala." Applying this similarly to other practices, they become a collection of activity practices for guru yoga.

Not being grateful is a sign of not valuing the Dharma. Without gratitude, all the efforts you do will be pointless and no qualities will arise in your mind stream. You will take that as a reason to cultivate wrong views, thinking—if you are audacious—that the guru could not possibly have any good qualities, or if you are somewhat less so, that other Dharma practitioners could not. You will have thus committed the first root downfall, and all the merit you have previously accumulated will be swept away as if with a broom.

If you remember the guru's kindness, dedication for him and the Dharma will naturally arise, and you will spontaneously develop all the positive qualities without effort. If true devotion does not come easily to you, you should gather as much merit as you can by offering to the Three Jewels, serving the Sangha, doing spiritual practice with your body and speech, and so forth. Then pray, "By accumulating this merit, may I come to develop extraordinary devotion to the guru." It is said that meditating this way will immediately produce devotion.

Those with the greatest devotion have the greatest spiritual practice. Those with average devotion have average practice, and the least devoted have the lowest spiritual practice. Naropa, Maitripa, Milarepa, Ja Yulwa, and others undertook great hardship for the sake of the guru and achieved siddhi through that alone. We cannot be like them.

Uncontrived devotion does not arise easily, so we are encouraged to train gradually, starting with supplication.

There are four factors for devotion to become the path:

1. Buddhajnana lost faith in Manjushri upon seeing that he was a householder with a wife, and this caused an obstacle preventing Buddhajnana from attaining supreme siddhi. Similarly, if you see the guru as having faults, the impurity of your own mind stream is to blame. How could buddhas have any faults? Let them do what they will. Even should you see them having sexual relations, telling lies, and so on, meditate thinking: "This is the best way to train disciples. Because of this, he will undoubtedly ripen and liberate many sentient beings, so this is a hundred, a thousand times more marvelous than keeping a pure moral code. He is not being deceptive or immoral. He alone is unmistaken about the highest conduct."

In particular, when he reprimands you, think that this extinguishes bad karma. If he slaps you, think he is driving away spirits and obstructors. Above all, think that due to his compassion, he is treating you as a father would a child and not being a false friend—he is very kind. If he seems displeased or does not pay attention to you, think that this is because your karmic obscurations have not been purified. Strive at the methods to purify your obscurations and please the guru by serving his body, speech, and mind. In brief, the first factor is not finding fault with the guru.

2. In the words of the Kagyu forefathers:

This authentic guru is precious—
Everything he does is excellent.
All of his deeds are qualities.

Even were he an executioner,
Just that would be beneficial; just that would be good.
It's certain he regards beings with compassion.

Even if he displays sexual misconduct and immorality,
His qualities increase; his qualities arise.
It is a sign of the union of means and prajna.

When he deceives others with lies,
He is guiding all beings on the path to liberation
Through various symbolic methods.

When he steals, seizes, or robs,
He transforms others' things into the accumulations
And pacifies the poverty of beings.

In actuality when such a guru
Reprimands you it is a wrathful mantra
Certain to dispel misfortunes and obstacles.

If he beats you, it is a blessing.
All siddhis arise from that.
All those with devotion take delight!

As this says, recognize that whatever he does is a positive quality. This is the second.

3. When meditating on devotion for the guru, forget being concerned about whether you are pleasing him or not in this life; do not even harbor hopes about whether or not you will achieve the supreme siddhi. Whether he accepts you with compassion or not, whether you achieve siddhi or not, there is nothing for you to do other than have devotion. Resolve to stop expecting or worrying. This is the third.

4. In the secular context, upstanding people are able to do anything for their bosses publicly, privately, and in between. That is for this life—for the sake of a few months or years. But we place our hopes in our gurus from now until we achieve enlightenment. Whatever of goodness and happiness arises in this life, the next, or in between—whether great

or small—it is solely the guru's kindness. Whatever spiritual qualities you develop depend only upon the guru, so focus all your actions of body, speech, and mind on serving him. With everything from your prayers for the guru to live long and for his activity to flourish on up, never be without an amenable and admiring attitude.

If you serve your guru with such attitudes, there is no way that your being will not be ripened and liberated.

For the training, everything is contained within two things: accomplish whatever the guru commands and do whatever he wishes. With your body, prostrate, circumambulate, write letters, sew, and run errands, or at the very least fetch water and sweep up. With your speech, recite prayers and praises to him, and tell others about his qualities. Answer questions in a way that pleases him and speak gently and respectfully without concealing your intentions. Do not speak even half a critical word about him, openly or in private. In your mind, cultivate devotion and pure view only, without falling into mistaken views for even an instant. Should something disagreeable happen to you due to bad karma arising and so forth, immediately catch it with mindfulness and never express it physically or verbally.

If due to previous bad karma you inadvertently go against his wishes, make your confession more intense by offering your body and possessions along with it. Exert yourself at confessing and vowing to refrain from repeating it by reciting the hundred syllables, amendment and confession offerings, and so forth. It is inappropriate to get along with, eat with, or even have conversations in an affectionate manner with those who go against your guru's wishes. It is taught that befriending those who demean your guru is no different from demeaning him yourself, even if you do not do so in actuality.

Materially, we should offer without reservation our guru the things that we treasure and whatever would please him. But we cull for ourselves the biggest and finest things that serve our purposes—be they horses, cattle, and what not—and offer the guru that which does not

suit us. We give ourselves a high title and ask for whichever empowerments, Dharma, and root instructions are the most sacred. If it does not
quite work out, we scowl with displeasure. We try to make him feel
grateful to us. We have no gratitude for the Dharma and key instructions he is able to grant us, but say we have done him a favor by requesting teachings and listening to him. Not understanding that offering the
guru possessions and service is for our own good, we try to show off and
gain status. It would be far better to just stay by ourselves than to do
anything like that.

Once you have developed true devotion, the signs of having received
the blessings will occur in actuality, as experiences, or in dreams, as
explained in the texts. Specifically, when the appearances of eight
worldly concerns dissipate, you put this life out of mind, the clear and
empty mind emerges nakedly, and realization suddenly arises, these are
the greatest, true signs. Whether or not you develop the meditation of
the actual practice depends upon this, so do not reach impatiently for
calm abiding and insight. Instead lay a firm foundation of good qualities in your being.

Instructions on the Main Practice

In general the secret words of the masters of experience and realization, the Kagyu forefathers, and *Mahamudra: The Ocean of Definitive Meaning* are a treasury of the profound true meaning, so read them respectfully. In particular, serve an authentic guru through the five methods of pleasing him and partake of the nectar of his speech.

The guru's words will appear vividly in your mind whereas reading books will yield only a dry understanding. Even if some experience arises, it will not give you confidence and will disappear in a few days. These two are completely different. However when you cannot find a qualified guru or are not able to serve him even if you do, collect many different types of instructions, and what is unclear in one will be clear in another. Then they will bring benefit when needed. In particular, since we do not know where our karmic connections lie, if you read the profound Dharma of all traditions with respect, a single word may unlock many meanings. Therefore read widely from the sutras and commentaries, and the understanding will bring great benefits suitable for your mind.

At such a time, some who imagine themselves great meditators do not serve a guru or do not refine their practice if they do. They never read texts of the oral instructions and would not understand them if they did. That kind of person is said to have impure karma. This seems to be the intention behind the criticism:

A fool's meditation on mahamudra
Will mostly cause birth as an animal.[51]

Others serve the guru, study, do retreat, and read many profound books, but it does not benefit them a whit. Their character gets wilder, their pride larger, and their eye of pure perception becomes more obscured. They spend all their time thinking about others' faults. Such people seem to be possessed by Mara.

There is no need for me who have no experience or realization to parrot the teachings of my forbearers, but in order to complete the text I shall write just enough about how to rest in calm abiding and insight so as to not leave the topic empty.

Generally, it is said, "Seek meditation through the view." First you determine the view through listening and contemplation. When you have gained certainty in the view, you rest in equipoise within its nature. However that meditation is far off for beginners, so it is not that profound.

In our Dakpo Kagyu tradition, it is said, "Seek the view through meditation." Without doing much analytical study and contemplation, you resolve the matter within the mind, and through this, the view naturally becomes realization. Thus it is a profound meditation that everyone, whether of sharp or dull faculties, can definitely put into practice.

In the tradition of Venerable Milarepa, when one has achieved stability in tummo and the illusory body,[52] the essence of mahamudra is naturally realized. Thus he taught the path of means[53] first. The peerless Gampopa taught his ordinary disciples mind training through the Kadampa stages of the path, and he taught his extraordinary disciples a brief version of the paths of means, followed by the sudden pointing-out instructions of mahamudra. Drogön Pakmodrupa emphasized the Fivefold Mahamudra, so the eight traditions in four pairs[54] practiced only the Fivefold Mahamudra. The Lord of Dharma Tsangpa Gyare, as well as Lorepa, Götsangpa, and others emphasized equal-taste. In any case, there is no difference in what they lead to, the realization of the nature of mahamudra.

Sentient beings of different capacities cannot be tamed by one deity or one Dharma. The Sage's teachings appear differently to people with different karma. Due to this, there are different interpretations of the philosophical schools, so they have various kinds of conduct. Those who see each other as non-Dharmic and criticize one another needlessly accumulate the karma of rejecting the Dharma. Each has its truth in its own context, so it is wrong to denigrate any of them. However their ultimate destination is this mahamudra alone.

To practice according to the Fivefold Mahamudra, first begin by going for refuge and generating bodhichitta according to the liturgy so that it is fully integrated into your being. Second, the vajrayana teachings, so called, are the two phases of creation and completion, so meditate on the creation phase with the four characteristics[55] by visualizing your body as any deity such as Vajra Varahi. Third, visualize your root guru on the crown of your head or in your heart and rouse intense devotion. Fourth, the main practice is to meditate on the actual practice, the union of calm abiding and insight. Fifth, seal your practice with dedication and aspiration without conceiving of the three spheres. There is not even one stage of the teachings of sutra and tantra that is not included in the Fivefold Mahamudra, so it is enough to practice this Dharma alone. Excessive complications are unnecessary. You might know all eighty-four thousand gates of Dharma, but if you do not practice them, at the time of death you will die an ordinary death.

Generally, at the time of gathering the accumulations and purifying obscurations, you should not limit yourself to one but practice whatever teachings you have seen or heard, like a famished person who sees food. Once you are certain about what to practice, do not think about or do anything else. Until you have a feeling for it, you must be persistent in one type of practice and be able to endure hardship.

As the method to develop samadhi, you must first practice calm abiding meditation. Just as the reflection of the moon in muddy water is unclear, a mind that is never free from thoughts even for an instant cannot recognize the wisdom of insight. Even if you grasp it hazily, you will not gain stability.

If beginners mix it with distraction, they cannot develop meditation, so solitude of the body and mind is necessary. Even if you cannot truly forget about this life, for the time being, do not bring any worldly affairs to mind at all. Think that whatever food and clothing you have will suffice, and do not worry about whether or not they will run out. With material things such as beds and so forth, make do with what you have—do not think, "This won't do, I must have one like that," or "This is not good enough; I should get that," and so on. Do not read books, write letters, or so forth unless absolutely necessary, and even then only a little. If you follow a thought, you will create a bad habit and eventually be unable to gain control. Avoid entirely meaningless conversations, questions and answers, and discussions. Do not worry about what might befall those close to you or speculate about where you might go in the future.

In short, go to a solitary place and cast aside entirely all the affairs of this life. As an auspicious condition for staying put, draw a swastika with chalk beneath your seat. Once you have set your place up, do not rearrange things. Arrange representations of the Three Jewels, mandalas, and other clean and pure offerings that will not distract you. Repeatedly make the intense commitment to never let your mind waver toward anything else until some experience has arisen, even if you should die, and make the Fivefold Mahamudra your main practice.

In calm abiding meditation, the posture and gaze are important, so sit in the vajra posture. Rest your hands in the mudra of equipoise four finger widths below your navel. Make your spine straight like an arrow. Square your shoulders. Tuck your chin slightly, towards the Adam's apple. Your lips neither open nor closed, touch your tongue to your upper palate, and let it rest naturally. With your eyes half open, look into the space eight finger-widths directly in front of your nose.

The points for the mind are to not follow the tracks of the past—do not think about anything that happened before. Do not anticipate the future—do not speculate at all about the good or bad things that might happen later. Let the present mind be without altering it. Do not expect meditation to arise or worry that it won't—do not be concerned and think, "Is this it or not?" Let the thought-free awareness of now settle in the nature of its own being without identifying, altering, disproving, or proving anything. Do not get distracted, do not meditate, do not alter it: All the points of how to settle the mind are complete in these three, and the three gates of liberation[56] are also exactly that.

Beginners should meditate for short sessions many times. When meditating, funnel your awareness and rest without getting distracted by anything. If a thought should suddenly occur, look vividly at its very essence. There is no need to block the thought, but do not follow it either. Even between sessions in post-meditation, apply the watchfulness of merely recognizing your nature and sustain that without getting distracted. Even when speaking, cooking, reading books, and so forth, apply watchfulness—in short, remain undistracted. At all times, whether in meditation or post-mediation, do not allow yourself to be distracted by sights and sounds on the outside or by the body and mind on the inside.

If you are too tight, that in itself will stimulate mental activity, so other than just letting it be and recognizing it, rest without binding yourself. You might have more thought activity than before, so that you get disturbed and are not at all interested in looking at your mind. Or you might rest tranquilly with no thoughts or agitation and thus feel very pleased. Sometimes while resting in that way, you might fall asleep, and sometimes you may breathe quite shallowly. You may spontaneously recognize dreams time and again. Sometimes while resting, a thought will occur, but as soon as it does, the mind will settle quietly. Or it may be as if after you retrieve the thought, you have something to place again. Such various kinds of experience occurring augurs well for knowing how to meditate, so if you maintain them without casting them aside, one of the types of calm abiding described in the texts—the high, middle, or low—will develop.

Although there are a great many ways for training in calm abiding with a support, concentrating on an image of Shakyamuni before you and counting the exhalations and inhalations of the breath are the most beneficial.

It is said that when consummate calm abiding has developed, all the defiled clairvoyances and miraculous abilities will arise. But people have varying qualities of channels as well as differences in their faculties. These days there is no one who can meditate on that level. Even if they could, this is a time when it is difficult to achieve the ordinary siddhis. Even if you could accomplish them, it is inappropriate to wish for them—they should arise incidentally. If clairvoyance and so forth happen to arise, just disregard them and let them go. Deliberately seeking them will only cause Mara to obstruct you. Similarly, it is said that this also produces fame, powers, and material wealth. But if those obstruct your spiritual practice, they are the blessings of Mara.

At this point, you will consider the mind resting serenely and the movement of discursive thought as separate. But this is only thinking "This is movement" or "This is stillness" and then looking at the nature. You do not yet know how to actually look at the nature, so this is called knowing stillness and movement.

Then just as waves and water are of one taste, without considering thought and awareness to be distinct and separate, rest in the self-aware, self-luminous nature. If you do not recognize this, place your attention vividly on the essence of the one who thinks, "This is stillness, this is movement." Apart from that, without any watching or analysis of mindfulness at all, rest serenely within the stillness.

By doing this, you may feel the satisfaction of continuous undistractedness, vividly clear and empty. Like snow falling on hot rocks, any thought that occurs will be caught as soon as it occurs. You may feel confidence in yourself but despair for others, thinking, "Why doesn't everyone mediate like this?" You may think, "If I stayed alone in the mountains, I could handle the solitude." It may be as if you no longer rely upon the eight worldly concerns. Sometimes a helter-skelter, willy-nilly feeling might come up and you won't find anything to focus on or anything to rest. Sometimes there may occur a dullness where you cannot say, "This is it," and so forth. These are all types of temporary experiences.

Then meticulously examine the mind again and again to determine where it comes from initially, where it goes in the end, and where it dwells in the meantime. Investigate its shape and color; whether it is single or multiple, and so on. It doesn't arise from anywhere. You cannot say, "It ceases here," and there is no place where it dwells in the present. There is no shape, color, or so forth to be discerned. Seeing clearly and nakedly the self-luminous essence of the mind that is free of all elaborations and has no object can be called insight, but this is just a taste of temporary experience and is not actually seeing the nature of realization. At this point, you will develop certainty that the seer and seen are not separate, and the thought will occur to you, "This is what resting without altering anything means."

There may be times you are unaware you have been distracted. Then mindful awareness returns all at once, and it becomes clear and bright. Or it will seem as if there is no focus to the meditation and you are just staying as you were, an ordinary person, so you wonder whether your meditation has gotten worse than before. Or even when thoughts occur, it may seem that you do not need to struggle as before and it is enough to just let it be as it is. Various such experiences—high, low, long lasting, and short—will occur. For a time, there will be no progress at all and you will get frustrated. Sometimes you will think there is no view or meditation superior to this. You might really want to discuss lofty realizations with others. You might also have dreams about siddhas from the past or yidam deities, or even sometimes about strange or evil things, making you hopeful, fearful, or suspicious.

Sometimes your practice might get mixed with distraction and you might think that distraction will not harm you, but if you are distracted for a long time, the five poisons and eight worldly concerns will rearise stronger than before. For a time, your mindfulness will not be able to keep up with them, and even if it does, it will be difficult to subdue distractions. Thus unless you have truly achieved stability, it is of the greatest importance to abandon distractions and become capable of meditating one-pointedly.

Then due to the blessings of devotion or something such as the awakening of previous karma, awareness is stripped bare. Without any need to recognize thoughts as they arise, the nature you look at and the person looking mix into one. You also no longer need to examine the appearances in the six consciousnesses, and you have nothing left to change in the awareness of your nature. Then other than entirely letting go of ordinary mind, you do not know how to describe it as any clarity, emptiness, or awareness that can be intellectually analyzed.

Then empty awareness, which is only slightly different from remaining in an ordinary state, will emerge relaxed. You will have thought that there is nothing about it you have not known from the very beginning, and you are astonished you have not recognized it till now. You will think that all the ways you previously pretended to look at the nature of mind were pointless thoughts.

You will also develop certainty in the Dharma and the guru, and you will be delighted with yourself. Though numerous distractions will still produce the appearances of the eight worldly concerns, from the moment mindfulness returns, you will not need to do much to correct it—just letting the mind be is enough. When this happens, it may seem that you should consider yourself to have partially realized your nature, but still that alone does not get you anywhere. So meditate till you die. Sacrifice food, clothing, and conversation. Let your heart be penetrated with devotion. Do not take even the slightest interest in the activities of this life. If you can do this, you will reach the end of your Dharma journey.

Lord Götsangpa said:

> Because I had intense devotion for the guru and was as diligent as if my hair had caught fire, I saw the nature of mind properly after twenty days. After three months, I was not affected by situations during the day, and after two years, that continued day and night.

Therefore if you have devotion and diligence, there is nothing that you cannot know or see.[57]

The text on mind training says, "Right now, practice the main points."[58] As this says, now at this time when we have gained a human body, the needs of future lives are more significant than this life. Practice is more significant than philosophy. And steadfastly meditating on the guru's instructions is the most significant.

Not being able to bear the suffering of practicing Dharma while being able to persevere through the hardships of accomplishing your interests in this life is wrong patience. Having no wish for the Dharma while wishing for the eight worldly concerns is wrong wishes. Not relishing the Dharma through listening, contemplating, and meditating while relishing material things is wrong relishing. Not feeling compassion for our own or others wrong actions while having compassion for hardships endured for the sake of Dharma is wrong compassion. Not bringing the people who depend on you to the Dharma while striving to benefit them in this life is wrong pursuits. Not rejoicing in virtuous deeds while rejoicing when misfortunes befall enemies is wrong rejoicing. Give up these six wrong ideas.

In particular, Nagarjuna taught:

> O Knower of the World, your mind should be
> Equanimous to the eight concerns:
> Gain and loss, pleasure and pain,
> Fame and oblivion, praise and scorn.[59]

It seems these eight worldly concerns, without being noticed, contaminate the beings of even those who imagine themselves genuine Dharma practitioners—what to speak of others—so it is important to subdue them at all costs.

Abandon in all respects the five wrong livelihoods—flattery, ingratiating yourself, hypocrisy, expropriating, and seeking gain through things. It would be best for us to develop qualities and high realization, but that is difficult. If we can just not shame ourselves or deceive others, and if we practice what we preach, that would be most wondrous.

There are said to be many pitfalls and deviations, but if you become able to cut through projections about the nature internally, then needless to say, you will truly be able to distinguish what are and what are not pitfalls and deviations. For those who hope for nonthought without getting to the heart of stillness and movement or for those who imagine that a conceptual glimpse of the nature of mind is the nature of mind, there is no need to wonder whether the pitfalls and deviations taught in the texts have arisen. In all practice, if there is no fixation, there will be no deviation. Here this only means extremely strong fixation on superiority—occasional slight fixation is not a deviation. It comes down to fixation and clinging at its basis.

The greatest deviations are treating your guru as an ordinary friend, having little pure perception of your Dharma friends, denigrating and slandering other schools, taking great pride in yourself, being hypocritical in your discipline, giving free rein to the five poisons, not respecting karmic cause and effect, mouthing the view and speaking often of emptiness, proclaiming your experiences in public, and 61lying about the highest human qualities[60] your main practice. However we have all been blessed by demons, and disciples have only the bad fortune of a degenerate age. Thus many—not knowing the crucial points of the Dharma—run after nothing but nonsense, and it seems that even Shakyamuni could not block the paths to pitfalls and deviations were he to try.

In short, the result of practicing Dharma should be that your mind is tamed, but most Dharma practitioners make their primary practice that which the Dharma teaches is wrong—fighting for the sake of Dharma, using the Dharma as an excuse for conflict, pretending to benefit others while profiting themselves, and so forth.

The peerless Gampopa said, "When you are a beginner, it is not a time to fight with the afflictions—it is the time to flee from them." We have not reached the level where we can take the afflicted as the path, so we must be cautious about alcohol, sex, anger, jealousy, careless sloth, and so forth. The ability to take afflictions as the path is said only about those like Telopa and Naropa whose ability to display miracles externally is a sign of having perfected the power of wisdom internally. It is not said about those whose polluted indulgence in the afflictions is a sign of not having control over their own minds. Those individuals who have no experience or realization at all in their beings may try to benefit sentient beings but are unable to, and harm themselves in addition. Just as the sprout of a great medicinal herb should be protected, not cut, being diligent in practice alone has the greatest benefit. It is said that those individuals who have not achieved stability in warmth may help others but will harm themselves. Once you have attained the bodhisattva levels, benefit for both yourself and others arises effortlessly.

When you encounter harm from illness, adversity, döns, obstructors, and so forth, look at the essence of the one who thinks, "I'm sick!" or "Döns are harming me!" When you are inexperienced, there may be no immediate effect, but with persistent repetition, eventually they will dissolve into emptiness and disappear without a trace. Then when their poisonous remnants reemerge, looking at the essence will decrease the intensity of clinging to illness, concepts of ghosts, and so forth. It is the same with suffering and so forth. If you are a bit more advanced than that, the occurrence of illness and so forth is not blocked but the essence is empty, naked, and distinct. But when you are not mindful, you are no different from an ordinary person.

You may understand that appearances are merely your own mind, but if you have not achieved confidence in your realization, when objects and mind meet, they will not be liberated as groundless and baseless. Thus for the time being, you should train in not grasping at whatever arises in the six consciousnesses. The best is to recognize them in the first instant. The next best is not to prolong them after the second instant but to continually apply the mindfulness of recognition. Telopa said:

> Appearances do not bind; fixation binds.
> Cut through attachment, Naropa.

In brief, thoughts are the natural energy of mind, like waves in water, so it is impossible for thoughts to vanish entirely. The various appearances to thought of objects such as form are like rainbows appearing in clear crystal. Thus no matter how high your realization, it is impossible that appearances will not occur. It all depends on whether you welcome thoughts and appearances with fixation or not.

If due to being undistracted, your recognition of your nature is continuous, no matter how many thoughts or appearances of objects there may be, they are said to be wisdom. If you do not recognize your nature, even nonthought is merely neutral. Once you recognize that what appears as thought is the natural expression of emptiness—appearance and emptiness indivisible—without any need to block thoughts this appears vividly as the empty essence and unceasing radiance. When this is aware of itself, it is called the inseparability of creation and completion, and that is enough.

When you persevere in practice, bad karma from the past may arise in unwanted ways as physical illness, mental suffering, and so forth. However just as stains appear when you wash a pot, this is a harbinger of your being becoming pure, it is said, so do not let your practice be snatched away by adversity; increase your diligence instead.

When you develop good qualities, which are signs of the path, do not try to distinguish whether they are genuine or obstacles of Mara. Even if they are genuine, they will immediately become obstacles of Mara if you overrate them. Therefore do not be attached to the good, do not be afraid of the bad—give up all expectation and worry.

Do not sit in a high position. Do not wear nice clothes. Do not collect fine things. Do not relish praise from others. Those are all conditions that give rise to pride. If you are always able to remain humble, there will be no way for arrogance and jealousy to arise. Hindrances do not occur until pride arises. When you think, "Even the guru has nothing better than this" or "Other monks do not know this much," and get prideful, hindrances will appear. Thus continually be devoted and have pure perception.

Having food that is too good produces attachment and afflictions, so only eat enough so as to not be hungry. If you receive food and clothing, do not pretend you do not need them. If you do not get them, do not particularly seek them. Be fine with whatever you get. Anything more than what keeps you from getting hungry or cold should be given to the gurus and Jewels. When training your mind such as by meditating on bodhichitta, there is no distinction of better or worse recipients, but when actually putting it into practice, beginners should choose the best recipients, the field of offerings.[61]

If you do not know when enough is enough with your desires, though you may be a practitioner in name, you are a fraud in actuality, so be content with anything. Having too many plans prevents you from integrating Dharma into your being, so you should repeatedly focus on what is immediate.

Whatever appears—mental stillness or movement, joy, pain or so forth—just sustain letting it be as it is, the free flow of the natural state. Do not block, establish, fix, or alter anything. With that as your basis, do your recitations of prayers and mantras, walking, pacing, lying down, sitting and so forth in such a state. This is known as spontaneous conduct. However until you achieve stability, you must guard your discipline like your own eyes. Respect and protect against even the subtlest karmic cause and effect. Otherwise you might base your confidence on a dry understanding of emptiness thinking, "Nothing will affect the nature." Paying lip service to practice, your behavior will become rough and crazy. It is possible some people with impure karma might see you as a siddha, but it is really the basis for ruining yourself and others, so it is important to be careful.

To summarize, though you may lack the fortune to be able to listen to, contemplate, and practice the scriptural traditions of the Buddha's words and the treatises, take the words of the Kagyu forefathers as your authority. When you do as much as you can, without getting lazy or discouraged, to follow their examples even a little bit, there is no doubt that the two benefits will spontaneously arise.

Therefore keep the basic vows and root samayas without any violations. Do not think that gathering the accumulations and purifying obscurations only partially is enough; strive as much as you can. Emphasize having few desires, being content, and being humble. Make devotion and pure perception central to your practice. Until you die, train without vacillating in the union of emptiness and compassion. As part of that, continually apply carefulness, mindfulness, and awareness. Through this, there will come a time when—with no need either for an introduction to the view and meditation or for many explanations of the levels and paths—the way things are, mahamudra, will arise from within. When you arrive at a state where there are no elaborations, doubts have been resolved, and expectations and worry have been exhausted, that is called achieving the result.

The path trod by the precious garland of Kagyus
From Vajradhara down to my root guru
Is profound Dharma with the warmth of blessings,
So striving to practice it accomplishes great aims.
May the nature ground mahamudra be awakened from the
     heart,
The stable unified path mahamudra be achieved,
And the natural face of result mahamudra be revealed—
May we achieve mighty Vajradhara in this life.
I wrote this not from desire for scholarship or fame
But on my guru's command. By the virtue gained,
May the teachings of the Practice Lineage flourish everywhere,
And may all who encounter it gain the perpetual domain of the
     natural state.

The Venerable Lama Karma Ösel Gyurme told me to write an easy-to-read, clear synopsis of the visualizations and meaning of the four preliminary practices of mahamudra. I respectfully agreed and wrote these as supporting notes to the Ninth Karmapa's *Ocean of Definitive Meaning*. Though I have no experience or realization, I have taken the words of the forefathers as an authority and not made up anything of my own. I, the false meditator Karma Ngawang Yönten Gyatso, wrote this in my thirty-first year at Künzang Dechen Ling, the most isolated retreat of Palpung. May it be beneficial to the teachings and beings. Virtue!

Translated by David Karma Choephel under the guidance of His Holiness the Gyalwang Karmapa Ogyen Trinley Dorje at Gyuto Monastery, Summer, 2014.

sGrub brgyud rin po che'i phreng ba
karma kaM tshang rtogs pa'i don rgyud las byung ba'i
gsung dri ma med pa rnams bkod nas
zhal 'don rgyun khyer gyi rim pa 'phags lam 'grod pa'i shing rta
zhes bya ba bzhugs so//

A Series of Daily Recitations
Compiled from the Stainless Words of the Succession of
Precious Masters of the Practice Lineage,
the Karma Kamtsang Meaning Lineage of Realization

རབ་དགའ་བ་ཡ་ག་ཏྲཱི་ལ་བ་ནོ་བ་ལེ་པ་ཐ།།

The Chariot That Travels the Noble Path

དཔལ་ལྡན་ཁྱབ་བདག་རྡོ་རྗེ་འཆང་དབང་རིགས་ཀུན་གཙོ་བོ་བླ་མ་གཙུག་ལ། །

དཀྱིལ་འཁོར་ཀུན་གྱི་འབྱུང་གནས་སྲིད་ཞིའི་དཔལ་གྱུར་ཡེ་དགའ་རྣལ་འབྱོར་མ། །

ཕྱིན་ལས་ཀུན་གྱི་བྱེད་པོར་དབང་བསྒྱུར་ཆོས་སྐྱོང་བེར་ཅན་ལྷམ་དྲལ་ལ། །

རྣལ་འབྱོར་ཆེ་གཅིག་གྱུས་པས་འདུད་དོ་འཕྲལ་མེད་ཐུགས་རྗེས་སྐྱོང་བར་མཛོད། །

སྒྲུབ་བརྒྱུད་རིན་པོ་ཆེ་ཡི་ལམ་སྲོལ་ལམས། །

བྱུང་བའི་ཐིན་རྣམས་རྒྱ་བོའི་རྒྱུན་ཆེན་པོ། །

བདག་གིས་བཤེས་གཉེན་མང་ལ་བསྟེན་བྱས་ཏེ། །

ཉམས་སུ་བླངས་ནས་བྱུང་རྒྱུ་སེམས་བསྐྱེད་ཕྱིན། །

རྡོ་རྗེའི་གསུང་རྣམས་གསལ་བཀོད་པ། །

འཕགས་ལམ་བགྲོད་པའི་ཤིང་རྟ་མཆོག །

ལམ་འདིར་ཞུགས་པའི་སྐལ་ལྡན་རྣམས། །

མ་ཡེངས་བརྩོན་འགྲུས་སྐྱེན་པར་མཛོད། །

དེ་ཡང་སྤྱིན་འགྲོའི་ཆོས་འདི་རྣམས་རྒྱུན་ཁྱེར་དུ་བྱེད་པའི་ཕྱིར་ཕུན་གྱི་ཇ་སྐབས་བསྐུལ་བའི་ཆེ་ནའང་ཕྱི་འདུལ་ཁིམས་ཀྱི་དགེ་སྲོང་དགེ་ཚུལ་དགེ་བསྙེན་གང་ཡིན་པའི་བསླབ་པ་དང་མཐུན་པས་ལྡང་བ། ནང་སྤྱིན་འདག་གི་བྱང་རྒྱུབ་སེམས་བསྐྱེད་དང་ཕྱིན་པས་འཚོགས་ལ་དགོན་མཆོག་གི་རྟེན་ལ་གུས་པས་ཕྱག་འཚལ། །གསང་བ་སྔགས་ཀྱི་རྡོ་རྗེ་སློབ་དཔོན་གྱི་བཀའན་དང་དམ་ཚིག་ལ་གནས་པས་བཞུགས་གྲལ་དུ་ཕྱུལ་བསམ་གཏན་གྱི་ཆོས་ལུ་དང་ཕྱིན་པས་འགྲོ། འདིག་རྟེན་ཆོས་བརྒྱད་ཀྱི་དབང་དུ་མ་སོང་བར་འཆི་ཆོས་ཡང་དག་པར་བྱེད་དོ་སྙམ་པས་ཞལ་འདོན་གྱི་དུས་སུཞང་རིག་པ་མ་ཡེངས་པར་སྐྱ་དོན་དབྱེར་མེད་དུ་མཉམ་པར་བཞག་ནས། །

To glorious Lord Vajradhara, master of all families, the guru Karmapa;
To the wellspring of all mandalas, the glory of existence and peace, the
    yidam Yogini;
To those with dominion over all activity, the protector Bernakchen and
    consort:
This yogi bows with wholehearted respect. Nurture me with your
    inseparable compassion.

Great is the current of the river of blessings flowing
From the tradition of the jewels of the Practice Lineage.
Many are the spiritual masters I have served,
And I have practiced and roused bodhichitta.

Thus I have arranged their vajra words clearly
In this great chariot that travels the noble path.
You fortunate ones who have entered this way
Be diligent and undistracted.

*In order to practice these preliminaries on a daily basis, when the drum
signals the beginning of a session, get up in accordance with the external
vinaya precepts, whether you are a bhikshu or novice, or hold the lay
precepts. Gather with the internal resolve of aspirational and engaged
bodhichitta, and bow respectfully to the representations of the Three Jewels.
Remaining within the commands of and samaya to the Vajra Master of the
secret mantra, sit in rows in the five-pointed posture of dhyana. Thinking
that you will practice the Dharma that is necessary at death, without
being influenced by the eight worldly concerns, rest properly in meditation
without distraction. While you recite, the words and meaning should be
inseparable.*

The Four Ordinary Preliminaries

ༀ མི་ལུས་དལ་འབྱོར་རྙེད་པར་དགའ་བའི་ཁྲིད་ཀྱི་ངག་འདོན་ནི།

The recitation for the instructions on the human body with its leisures and resources, so difficult to find:

དང་པོ་བསྒོམ་བྱ་དལ་འབྱོར་རིན་ཆེན་འདི། །

dang po gom ja dal jor rin chen di
First meditate on this precious human body,

ཐོབ་དཀའ་འཇིག་སླ་ད་རེས་དོན་ཡོད་བྱ། །

top ka jik la da re dön yö ja
So difficult to gain, so easy to lose.
This time I shall make it meaningful!

འཆི་བ་མི་རྟག་པ་ནི།

Death and impermanence:

གཉིས་པ་སྣོད་བཅུད་ཐམས་ཅད་མི་རྟག་ཅིང་། །

nyi pa nö chü tam che mi tak ching
Second, the world and living beings are transient,

སྒོས་སུ་འགྲོ་བའི་ཚེ་སྲོག་ཆུ་བུར་འདྲ། །

gö su dro way tse sok chu bur dra
Especially my life, like a water bubble—

ནམ་འཆི་ཆ་མེད་འཆི་ཚེ་རོ་རུ་འགྱུར། །

nam chi cha me chi tse ro ru gyur
Who knows when I will die and become a corpse?

དེ་ལ་ཆོས་ཀྱི་ཕན་ཕྱིར་བརྩོན་པས་བསྒྲུབ། །

de la chö kyi pen chir tsön pay drup
Since Dharma will help then, I'll practice diligently.

ལས་རྒྱུ་འབྲས་ནི།

Karmic cause and effect

གསུམ་པ་ཤི་ཚེ་རང་དབང་མི་འདུ་བར། །

sum pa shi tse rang wang mi du war

Third, there is no freedom at the time of death.

ལས་ནི་བདག་གིར་བྱ་ཕྱིར་སྡིག་པ་སྤང་། །

le ni dak gir ja chir dik pa pang

In order to gain control over karma,

དགེ་བའི་བྱ་བས་རྟག་ཏུ་འདའ་བར་བྱ། །

ge way ja way tak tu da war ja

I'll give up misdeeds and always do virtuous acts.

ཞེས་བསམས་ཉིན་རེ་རང་རྒྱུད་ཉིད་ལ་བརྟག །

she sam nyin re rang gyü nyi la tak

Thinking thus, I'll examine myself every day.

འཁོར་བའི་ཉེས་དམིགས་ནི།

The defects of samsara:

བཞི་པ་འཁོར་བའི་གནས་གྲོགས་བདེ་འབྱོར་སོགས། །

shi pa khor way ne drok de jor sok

Fourth, the places, friends, pleasures, and riches of samsara

སྡུག་བསྔལ་གསུམ་གྱིས་རྟག་ཏུ་མནར་བའི་ཕྱིར། །

duk ngel sum gyi tak tu ngar way chir

Are always stricken with the three sufferings,

གསོད་སར་ཁྲིད་པའི་གཤེད་མའི་དགའ་སྟོན་ལྟར། །

sö sar tri pay she may ga tön tar

Like the last feast before an execution.

ཞེན་འཁྲིས་བཅད་ནས་བརྩོན་པས་བྱང་ཆུབ་བསྒྲུབ། །

shen tri che ne tsön pay jang chup drup

Cutting the ties of attachment, I'll strive to reach enlightenment.

ཞེས་པས་ཕུན་ཚོང་གི་སྟོན་འགྲོ་བཞི་དང་།།

Refuge and Bodhichitta

ༀ དེ་ནས་རྒྱུད་སྟོད་དུ་རུང་ཞིང་ཅེ་བྱུས་བར་བའི་ལམ་དུ་འགྲོ་བ་སྐྱབས་འགྲོ་སེམས་བསྐྱེད་ཁྲིད་ཀྱི་
འདོན་བྱ་ནི།

Next, the recitation for the instructions on refuge and bodhichitta, which makes your being into a suitable vessel and brings all you do onto the path of liberation:

མདུན་དུ་མཚོ་དབུས་དཔག་བསམ་ལྗོན་ཤིང་གི །

dün du tso ü pak sam jön shing gi
Before me in the center of a lake

སྡོང་པོ་རྩ་བ་གཅིག་ལ་ཡལ་ག་ལྔ། །

dong po tsa wa chik la yal ga nga
There is a wish-fulfilling tree that has

རྒྱས་པའི་དབུས་མར་སེང་ཁྲི་པདྨ་དང་། །

gye pay ü mar seng tri pe ma dang
A single trunk from which there spread five limbs.

ཉི་ཟླའི་སྟེང་དུ་རྩ་བའི་བླ་མ་ནི། །

nyi day teng du tsa way la ma ni
In its center on a lion throne and cushion
Of lotus, sun, and moon is my root guru,

རྡོ་རྗེ་འཆང་ལ་བཀའ་བརྒྱུད་བླ་མས་བསྐོར། །

dor je chang la ka gyü la may kor
Great Vajradhara amidst the Kagyu lamas.

མདུན་དུ་ཡི་དམ་གཡས་སུ་སངས་རྒྱས་དང་། །

dün du yi dam ye su sang gye dang
Yidams in front and Buddhas to the right;

རྒྱབ་ཏུ་དམ་ཆོས་གཡོན་དུ་དགེ་འདུན་དང་། །

gyap tu dam chö yön du gen dün dang
Dharma behind, the Sangha to the left.

གདན་ཁྲིའི་འོག་ཏུ་ཆོས་སྐྱོང་སྲུང་མ་རྣམས། །

den triy ok tu chö kyong sung ma nam
Beneath the throne are the Dharma protectors.

སོ་སོའི་རིགས་མཐུན་འཁོར་ཚོགས་རྒྱ་མཚོས་བསྐོར། །

so soy rik tün khor tsok gya tsoy kor
Each is amidst an ocean of their kind.

མཚོ་མཐའི་ནེའུ་སེང་སྟེང་དུ་མཁའ་ཁྱབ་ཀྱི། །

tso tay neu seng teng du kha khyap kyi
And in the meadows on the lake shores are

མ་རྒན་ཐམས་ཅད་འབོད་པར་གྱུར་པ་ལས། །

ma gen tam che khö par gyur pa le
All of my former mothers, filling space.

ཙེ་གཅིག་ཡིད་ཀྱིས་སྐྱབས་འགྲོ་སེམས་བསྐྱེད་གྱུར། །

tse chik yi kyi kyap dro sem kye gyur
Wholeheartedly we go for refuge and rouse bodhichitta.

བདག་དང་ནམ་མཁའི་མཐའ་དང་མཉམ་པའི་སེམས་ཅན་ཐམས་ཅད་ཕྱོགས་

dak dang nam khay ta dang nyam pay sem chen tam che chok
I and all sentient beings equal to the reaches of space go for refuge

བཅུ་དུས་གསུམ་གྱི་དེ་བཞིན་གཤེགས་པ་ཐམས་ཅད་ཀྱི་སྐུ་གསུང་ཐུགས་ཡོན་

chu dü sum gyi de shin shek pa tam che kyi ku sung tuk yön
to the great and glorious gurus including our kind root guru and

ཏན་ཕྲིན་ལས་ཐམས་ཅད་གཅིག་ཏུ་བསྡུས་པའི་ངོ་བོར་གྱུར་པ།

ten trin le tam che chik tu dü pay ngo wor gyur pa
lineage gurus—those who are the essence of all the body, speech,

ཆོས་ཀྱི་ཕུང་པོ་སྟོང་ཕྲག་བརྒྱད་ཅུ་རྩ་བཞིའི་འབྱུང་གནས་འཕགས་པའི་དགེ་

chö kyi pung po tong trak gye chu tsa shiyi jung ne pak pay gen
mind, qualities, and activity of all the tathagatas of the ten directions

འདུན་ཐམས་ཅད་ཀྱི་མངའ་བདག །དྲིན་ཅན་རྩ་བ་དང་བརྒྱུད་པར་བཅས་པའི་

dün tam che kyi nga dak   drin chen tsa wa dang gyü par che pay
and three times combined into one, the wellspring of the eighty-four

དཔལ་ལྡན་བླ་མ་རྣམས་ལ་སྐྱབས་སུ་མཆིའོ། །

pal den la ma nam la kyap su chi o
thousand aggregates of Dharma, and lords of all the noble Sanghas.

ཡི་དམ་དཀྱིལ་འཁོར་གྱི་ལྷ་ཚོགས་རྣམས་ལ་སྐྱབས་སུ་མཆིའོ། །

yi dam kyil khor gyi lha tsok nam la kyap sum chi o

We go for refuge to the yidams, the gatherings of deities in the mandalas.

སངས་རྒྱས་བཅོམ་ལྡན་འདས་རྣམས་ལ་སྐྱབས་སུ་མཆིའོ། །

sang gye chom den de nam la kyap sum chi o

We go for refuge to the bhagavan buddhas.

དམ་པའི་ཆོས་རྣམས་ལ་སྐྱབས་སུ་མཆིའོ། །

dam pay chö nam la kyap sum chi o

We go for refuge to the True Dharma.

འཕགས་པའི་དགེ་འདུན་རྣམས་ལ་སྐྱབས་སུ་མཆིའོ། །

pak pay gen dün nam la kyap sum chi o

We go for refuge to the noble sanghas.

དཔའ་བོ་མཁའ་འགྲོ་ཆོས་སྐྱོང་སྲུང་མའི་ཚོགས་ཡེ་ཤེས་ཀྱི་སྤྱན་དང་ལྡན་པ

pa wo khan dro chö kyong sung may tsok ye she kyi chen dang den

We go for refuge to the gatherings of heroes, dakinis, Dharma

རྣམས་ལ་སྐྱབས་སུ་མཆིའོ། །

pa nam la kyap sum chi o

protectors, and guardians who have the eye of wisdom.

བདུན་ནམ་ཉེར་གཅིག་གམ་ཅི་ནུས་བཟླད།

Recite this seven, twenty-one, or as many times as possible.[62]

རྗེ་བྱང་ཆུབ་སྙིང་པོར་མཆིས་ཀྱི་བར། །

jang chup nying por chi kyi bar
Until I reach enlightenment's essence,

སངས་རྒྱས་རྣམས་ལ་སྐྱབས་སུ་མཆི། །

sang gye nam la kyab su chi
I go for refuge to the buddhas.

ཆོས་དང་བྱང་ཆུབ་སེམས་དཔའ་ཡི། །

chö dang jang chub sem pa yi
I go for refuge to the Dharma,

ཚོགས་ལ་འང་དེ་བཞིན་སྐྱབས་སུ་མཆི། །

tsok la'ang de shin kyab su chi
And Sangha of bodhisattvas, too.

ཇི་ལྟར་སྔོན་གྱི་བདེ་གཤེགས་ཀྱིས། །

ji tar ngön gyi de shek kyi
Just as the sugatas of the past

བྱང་ཆུབ་ཐུགས་ནི་བསྐྱེད་པ་དང་། །

jang chup tuk ni kye pa dang
Aroused the mind of bodhichitta;

བྱང་ཆུབ་སེམས་དཔའི་བསླབ་པ་ལ། །

jang chup sem pay lap pa la
Just as they followed step-by-step

དེ་དག་རིམ་བཞིན་གནས་པ་ལྟར། །

de dak rim shin ne pa tar

The training of the bodhisattvas,

དེ་བཞིན་འགྲོ་ལ་ཕན་དོན་དུ། །

de shin dro la pen dön du

So too shall I, to benefit wanderers,

བྱང་ཆུབ་སེམས་ནི་བསྐྱེད་བགྱི་ཞིང་། །

jang chup sem ni kye gyi shing

Arouse the mind of bodhichitta.

དེ་བཞིན་དུ་ནི་བསླབ་པ་ལའང་། །

de shin du ni lap pa la

So too shall I follow step-by-step

རིམ་པ་བཞིན་དུ་བསླབ་པར་བགྱི། །

rim pa shin du lap par gyi (3x)

The bodhisattvas' training.

ཞེས་ལན་གསུམ།

Three times.

དེང་དུས་བདག་ཚེ་འབྲས་བུ་ཡོད། །

deng dü dak tse dre bu yö
My life has become fruitful now;

མི་ཡི་སྲིད་པ་ལེགས་པར་ཐོབ། །

mi yi si pa lek par top
I have gained this human existence well.

དེ་རིང་སངས་རྒྱས་རིགས་སུ་སྐྱེས། །

de ring sang gye rik su kye
Today I'm born in the Buddha's family—

སངས་རྒྱས་སྲས་སུ་བདག་དེང་གྱུར། །

sang gye se su dak deng gyur
I've now become the Buddha's child.

ད་ནི་བདག་གིས་ཅི་ནས་ཀྱང་། །

da ni dak gi chi ne kyang
In every case I'll always act

རིགས་དང་མཐུན་པའི་ལས་བཙམས་ཏེ། །

rik dang tün pay le tsam te
In ways that befit my family

སྐྱོན་མེད་བཙུན་པའི་རིགས་འདི་ལ། །

kyön me tsün pay rik di la
So that I bring no blemish on

 རྟོག་པར་མི་འགྱུར་དེ་ལྟར་བྱ། །

nyok par mi gyur de tar ja
This flawless, venerable family.

བདག་གིས་དེ་རིང་སྐྱོབ་པ་ཐམས་ཅད་ཀྱི། །

dak gi de ring kyop pa tam che kyi
Today in the presence of all the protectors

སྤྱན་སྔར་འགྲོ་བ་བདེ་གཤེགས་ཉིད་དང་ནི། །

chen nga dro wa de shek nyi dang ni
I invite all sentient beings as my guests

བར་དུ་བདེ་ལ་མགྲོན་དུ་བོས་སིན་གྱིས། །

bar du de la drön du bö sin gyi
To buddhahood, and till then happiness.

ལྷ་དང་ལྷ་མིན་ལ་སོགས་དགའ་བར་གྱིས། །

lha dang lha min la sok ga war gyi
Gods, demigods, and everyone rejoice!

བྱང་ཆུབ་སེམས་ནི་རིན་པོ་ཆེ། །

jang chup sem ni rin po che
May bodhichitta, great and precious,

མ་སྐྱེས་པ་རྣམས་སྐྱེས་གྱུར་ཅིག །

ma kye pa nam kye gyur chik
Arise where it has not arisen.

སྐྱེས་པ་ཉམས་པ་མེད་པ་དང་། །

kye pa nyam pa me pa dang
Never weakening where it has arisen,

གོང་ནས་གོང་དུ་འཕེལ་བར་ཤོག །

gong ne gong du pel war shok
May it grow ever more and more.

བྱང་ཆུབ་སེམས་དང་མི་འབྲལ་ཞིང་། །

jang chup sem dang min dral shing
Never parted from bodhichitta,

བྱང་ཆུབ་སྤྱོད་ལ་གཞོལ་བ་དང་། །

jang chup chö la shöl wa dang
May I strive toward enlightened conduct

སངས་རྒྱས་རྣམས་ཀྱིས་ཡོངས་བཟུང་ཞིང་། །

sang gye nam kyi yong sung shing
And be accepted by the Buddhas.

བདུད་ཀྱི་ལས་རྣམས་སྤོང་བར་ཤོག །

duu kyi le nam pong war shok
May I give up the acts of maras.

བྱང་ཆུབ་སེམས་པ་དཔའ་རྣམས་ཀྱིས་ནི། །

jang chup sem pa nam kyi ni
May I accomplish the intentions

116

འགྲོ་དོན་ཐུགས་ལ་དགོངས་འགྲུབ་ཤོག །

dro dön tuk la gong drup shok
Of bodhisattvas for beings' benefit.

མགོན་པོ་ཡིས་ནི་གང་དགོངས་པ། །

gön po yi ni gang gong pa
May sentient beings be endowed

སེམས་ཅན་རྣམས་ལ་དེ་འབྱོར་ཤོག །

sem chen nam la de jor shok
With whatever the protectors intend.

སེམས་ཅན་ཐམས་ཅད་བདེ་དང་ལྡན་གྱུར་ཅིག །

sem chen tam che de dang den gyur chik
May every sentient being be happy,

ངན་འགྲོ་ཐམས་ཅད་རྟག་ཏུ་སྟོངས་པར་ཤོག །

ngen dro tam che tak to tong par shok
All lower realms forever empty.

བྱང་ཆུབ་སེམས་པ་གང་དག་སར་བཞུགས་པ། །

jang chup sem pa gang dak sar shuk pa
May I fulfill the wishes of all

དེ་དག་ཀུན་གྱི་སྨོན་ལམ་འགྲུབ་པར་ཤོག །

de dak kün gyi mön lam drup par shok
The bodhisattvas on pure levels.

སེམས་ཅན་ཐམས་ཅད་བདེ་བ་དང་བདེ་བའི་རྒྱུ་དང་ལྡན་པར་གྱུར་ཅིག །

sem chen tam che de wa dang de way gyu dang den par gyur chik
May all sentient beings be happy and have the causes of happiness.

སྡུག་བསྔལ་དང་སྡུག་བསྔལ་གྱི་རྒྱུ་དང་བྲལ་བར་གྱུར་ཅིག །

duk ngel dang duk ngel gyi gyu dang dral war gyur chik
May they be free of suffering and the causes of suffering.

སྡུག་བསྔལ་མེད་པའི་བདེ་བ་དམ་པ་དང་མི་འབྲལ་བར་གྱུར་ཅིག །

duk ngel me pay de wa dam pa dang min dral war gyur chik
May they never be parted from the highest joy, free of suffering.

ཉེ་རིང་ཆགས་སྡང་གཉིས་དང་བྲལ་བའི་བཏང་སྙོམས་ཆེན་པོ་ལ་གནས་པར་

nye ring chak dang nyi dang dral way tang nyom chen po la ne par
May they dwell in the great equanimity free of attachment or hatred for

གྱུར་ཅིག །

gyur chik
those near or far.

ཐ་མར་སྐྱབས་ཡུལ་འོད་ཞུ་བདག་དང་འདྲེས། །

ta mar kyap yül ö shu dak dang dre
At the end, the sources of refuge melt into light and mix into me.

The Meditation and Recitation of Vajrasattva

༈ ཕྱག་སྐྱེབ་དག་པར་བྱེད་པ་རྡོ་རྗེ་སེམས་དཔའི་བསྒོམ་བཟླས་ནི།

The meditation and recitation of vajrasattva, which purifies misdeeds and obscurations

རང་གི་སྤྱི་བོར་པད་ཟླའི་གདན་གྱི་སྟེང་། །

rang gi chi wor pe day den gyi teng
Above my crown upon a lotus and moon seat

བླ་མ་རྡོ་རྗེ་སེམས་དཔའ་རྒྱན་ལྡན་དཀར། །

la ma dor je sem pa gyen den kar
Is Guru Vajrasattva, white, with ornaments,

ཞལ་གཅིག་ཕྱག་གཉིས་གཡས་པས་རྡོ་རྗེ་དང་། །

shal chik chak nyi ye pay dor je dang
One face, two arms. His right hand holds a vajra;

གཡོན་པས་དྲིལ་བུ་འཛིན་ཅིང་སྐྱིལ་ཀྲུང་བཞུགས། །

yön pay dril bu dzin ching kyil trung shuk
His left, a bell. He sits in vajra posture.

ཕྱགས་ཀའི་འོད་ཟེར་གྱིས་ཡེ་ཤེས་པའི་ཚོགས་སྤྱན་དྲངས་ཏེ་བསྟིམ་པས་དཀོན་མཆོག་ཀུན་འདུས་ཀྱི་རྡོ་བོར་བསྒོམ་ལ། དག་ཏུ།

Meditate that light from his heart invites the gatherings of wisdom beings, who dissolve into him so that he becomes the embodiment of all the jewels. Recite:

བླ་མ་རྡོ་རྗེ་སེམས་དཔའ་རང་གཞན་ནམ་མཁའི་མཐའ་དང་མཉམ་པའི་སེམས་

la ma dor je sem pa rang shen nam khay ta dang nyam pay sem
Recite: Guru Vajrasattva, I beseech you to cleanse and purify all the

ཅན་ཐམས་ཅད་ཀྱི་སྡིག་སྒྲིབ་ཉེས་ལྟུང་གི་ཚོགས་ཐམས་ཅད་བྱང་ཞིང་དག་པར་

chen tam che kyi dik drip nye tung gi tsok tam che jang shing dak
misdeeds, obscurations, wrongs, and downfalls of myself and all

མཛད་དུ་གསོལ། གསོལ་བ་བཏབ་པས་རྡོར་སེམས་ཀྱི་ཐུགས་ཀར་ཟླ་བའི་

par dze du söl   söl wa tap pay dor sem kyi tuk kar da way
other beings throughout space. Due to my prayer, nectar from a HŪM

སྟེང་དུ་ཧཱུྃ་གི་མཐར་ཡི་གེ་བརྒྱ་པས་བསྐོར་བ་ལས་བདུད་རྩིའི་རྒྱུན་བྱུང་བ་

teng du hung gi tar yi ge gya pay kor wa le dü tsiy gyün jung wa
surrounded by the hundred syllables on a moon in Vajrasattva's heart flows

དང་། སྐུ་ལས་བདུད་རྩི་བབས། བདག་གི་ཚངས་བུག་ནས་ཞུགས་ལུས་གང་

dang   ku le dü tsi bap   dak gi tsang puk ne suk lü gang
down from his body. It enters me through my fontanel, filling my body

བས་སྡིག་སྒྲིབ་ཉེས་ལྟུང་ཐམས་ཅད་དག་པར་གྱུར།

way dik drip nye tung tam che dak par gyur
and purifying all my misdeeds, obscurations, wrongs, and downfalls.

ༀ་བཛྲ་ས་ཏྭ་ས་མ་ཡ། མ་ནུ་པྰ་ལ་ཡ། བཛྲ་ས་ཏྭ་ཏྭེ་ནོ་པ་ཏིཥྛ་ཌྲྀ་ཌྷོ

oṃ vajrasatva samayamanupālaya   vajrasatva tvenopatiṣṭha dṛidho

OṂ VAJRASATVA SAMAYAM ANUPĀLAYA VAJRASATVA TVENOPATIṢṬHA

མེ་བྷ་ཝ། སུ་ཏོ་ཥྱོ་མེ་བྷ་ཝ། སུ་པོ་ཥྱོ་མེ་བྷ་ཝ། ཨ་ནུ་རཀྟོ

me bhava   sutoṣhyo me bhava   supoṣhyo me bhava   anurakto

DṚIḌHO ME BHAVA SUTOṢHYO ME BHAVA SUPOṢHYO ME BHAVA ANURAKTO

མེ་བྷ་ཝ། སརྦ་སིདྡྷིཾ་མྦེ་པྲ་ཡཙྪ། སརྦ་ཀརྨ་སུ་ཙ་མེ

me bhava   sarva siddhim me prayaccha   sarva-karmasu cha me

ME BHAVA SARVA SIDDHIM ME PRAYACCHA SARVA-KARMASU CHA ME

ཙིཏྟཾ་ཤྲེ་ཡཿ་ཀུ་རུ་ཧཱུྃ་ཧ་ཧ་ཧ་ཧོཿ བྷ་ག་ཝཱན། སརྦ་

chittaṃ shreyaḥ kuru hūṃ ha ha ha ha hoḥ   bhagavān   sarva-

CHITTAṂ SHREYAḤ KURU HŪṂ HA HA HA HA HOḤ BHAGAVĀN SARVA-

ཏ་ཐཱ་ག་ཏ་བཛྲ་མཱ་མེ་མུཉྩ་བཛྲཱི་བྷ་ཝ་མ་ཧཱ་ས་མ་ཡ་ས་ཏྭ་ཨཱཿ

tathāgata vajra mā me muñcha vajrī bhava mahāsamayasatva āḥ

TATHĀGATA VAJRA MĀ ME MUÑCHA VAJRĪ BHAVA MAHĀSAMAYASATVA ĀḤ

ༀ་བཛྲ་ས་ཏྭ་ཧཱུྃ།

oṃ vajrasatva hūṃ

OṂ VAJRASATVA HŪṂ

ཞེས་ཡིག་བརྒྱ་དང་ཡི་གེ་དྲུག་པ་ཅི་ནུས་བཟླས། མཐར་ཐལ་མོ་སྙིང་གར་སྦྱར་ཏེ།

Recite as many as you are able. At the end, join your palms at your heart:

121

མགོན་པོ་བདག་ནི་མི་ཤེས་རྨོངས་པ་ཡིས། །

gön po dak ni mi she mong pa yi

Protector, out of ignorant delusion,

དམ་ཚིག་ལ་ནི་འགལ་ཞིང་ཉམས། །

dam tsk la ni gal shing nyam

I've broken and transgressed samaya.

བླ་མ་མགོན་པོས་སྐྱབས་མཛོད་ཅིག །

la ma gön poy kyap dzö chik

Guardian guru, please protect me!

གཙོ་བོ་རྡོ་རྗེ་འཛིན་པ་སྟེ། །

tso wo dor je dzin pa kye

O vajra holder who in essence

ཐུགས་རྗེ་ཆེན་པོའི་བདག་ཉིད་ཅན། །

tuk je chen poy dak nyi chen

Are great compassion, foremost of

འགྲོ་བའི་གཙོ་ལ་བདག་སྐྱབས་ཆི། །

dro way tso la dak kyap chi

All beings, I go to you for refuge.

སྐུ་གསུང་ཐུགས་རྩ་བ་དང་ཡན་ལག་གི་དམ་ཚིག་ཉམས་ཆགས་ཐམས་ཅད

ku sung tuk tsa wa dang yen lak gi dam tsik nyam chak tam che

I admit and confess all violations of the root and secondary samayas of

མཐོལ་ལོ་བཤགས་སོ། །སྡིག་སྒྲིབ་ཉེས་ལྟུང་གི་ཚོགས་ཐམས་ཅད་བྱང་ཞིང་

to lo shak so   dik drip nye tung gi tsok tam che jang shing
body, speech, and mind. I ask you to bless me so that all my misdeeds,

དག་པར་བྱིན་གྱིས་བརླབ་ཏུ་གསོལ།

dak par jin gyi lap to söl
obscurations, wrongs, and downfalls be cleansed and purified.

རྡོ་རྗེ་སེམས་དཔས་བདག་ལ་དབུགས་དབྱུང་ནས། །

dor je sem pay dak la uk chung ne
Vajrasattva grants me relief, melts into light,

འོད་ཞུ་བདག་ལ་ཐིམ་པས་གཉིས་མེད་གྱུར། །

ö shu dak la tim pay nyi me gyur
And dissolves into me, becoming inseparable.

Mandala Offerings

ༀ ཚོགས་གཉིས་རྫོགས་པར་བྱེད་པའི་བྱེར་མཎྜལ་ནི།

Mandala offerings, which perfect the two accumulations

སྒྲུབ་པའི་མཎྜལ་ཡོད་ན་དེ་ཉིད་ནི། བྷྲཱུཾ་ལས་གཞལ་ཡས་ཁང་དུ་ཚོམ་བུ་ལྔ་དཀོན་མཆོག་ལྔར་བསྒྱེད།

If you have a mandala of accomplishment, visualize that from a BHRŪṂ
there is a palace, in which the five piles are the five jewels.

མདུན་གྱི་ནམ་མཁའི་དབུས་སུ་བླ་མ་དང་། །

dün gyi nam khay ü su la ma dang
In the center of the sky before me are the gurus

མདུན་གཡས་རྒྱབ་དང་གཡོན་དུ་རིམ་པ་བཞིན། །

dün ye gyap dang yön du rim pa shin
And to their front, right, back, and left respectively

ཡི་དམ་སངས་རྒྱས་ཆོས་དང་དགེ་འདུན་དང་། །

yi dam sang gye chö dang gen dün dang
Are the yidams, buddhas, dharma, and the sangha

རང་རིགས་འཁོར་བཅས་གཞན་ཡང་གདན་མཆམས་སུ། །

rang rik khor che shen yang den tsam su
With retinues of their own kind; between the seats,

ཆོས་སྐྱོང་རྒྱ་མཚོ་ལ་སོགས་དཀོན་མཆོག་རྣམས། །

chö kyong gya tso la sok kön chok nam
An ocean of Dharma protectors. In the presence

ཚོགས་ཀྱི་ཞིང་མཆོག་དམ་པ་བཞུགས་པའི་དྲུང་། །

tsok kyi shing chok dam pa shuk pay drung
Of these—the Jewels, the supreme field of accumulations:

མཆོད་པའི་མཎྜལ་ལག་ཏུ་བླངས་ནས་རྡུལ་གཙང་ཞིང་དག་པར་ཕྱི་བའི་ཚེ། གཉུང་འཛིན་གྱིས་
བསྒྲུབས་པའི་བདག་གཞན་རྒྱུད་ཀྱི་སྡིག་སྒྲིབ་དག་པར་བསམ། ཚིག་འདོན་ཞིང་དོན་གསལ་འདེབས་
པ་དང་། ཚོས་སུ་བཀོད་ནས་འབུལ་བ་རྣམས་ཕྱོགས་མཐུན་དུ་སྟེ།

*Pick up the mandala of offering, and as you wipe it to clean and purify
it of dust, think that the dualistic misdeeds and obscurations in your own
and others' mind streams are purified. Recite the hundred syllables* OM
VAJRASATVA… *Recite the words and visualize the meaning while placing
the offerings in the appropriate directions:*

ཨོཾ་བཛྲ་བྷུ་མི་ཨཱཿ་ཧཱུྃ།

oṃ vajra bhūmi āḥ hūṃ

OṂ VAJRA BHŪMI ĀḤ HŪṂ

གཞི་རྣམ་པར་དག་པ་དབང་ཆེན་གསེར་གྱི་ས་གཞི།

shi nam par dak pa wang chen ser gyi sa shi
The ground is the powerful golden earth.

ཨོཾ་བཛྲ་རེ་ཁེ་ཨཱཿ་ཧཱུྃ།

oṃ vajra rekhe āḥ hūṃ

OṂ VAJRA REKHE ĀḤ HŪṂ

ཕྱི་ལྕགས་རིའི་འཁོར་ཡུག་གི་ར་བས་ཡོངས་སུ་བསྐོར་བའི་དབུས་སུ་རིའི

chi chak riyi khor yuk gi ra way yong su kor way ü su riyi
The outside is encircled by a ring of iron mountains. In the center is the

རྒྱལ་པོ་རི་བོ་མཆོག་རབ། ཤར་ལུས་འཕགས་པོ། ལྷོ་འཛམ་བུ་གླིང་།

gyal po ri wo chok rap   shar lü pak po   lho dzam bu ling
king of mountains, Mount Meru. To the east is Superior Body, to the

ནུབ་བ་ལང་སྤྱོད། བྱང་སྒྲ་མི་སྙན། ལུས་དང་ལུས་འཕགས།

nup ba lang chö   jang dra mi nyen   lü dang lü pak
south Rose Apple Land, to the west Bountiful Cow, and to the north

རྔ་ཡབ་དང་རྔ་ཡབ་གཞན། གཡོ་ལྡན་དང་ལམ་མཆོག་འགྲོ།

nga yap dang nga yap shen   yo den dang lam chok dro
Unpleasant Sound. Deha and Videha, Chāmara and Avara, Śhaṭhā and

སྒྲ་མི་སྙན་དང་སྒྲ་མི་སྙན་གྱི་ཟླ། རིན་པོ་ཆེའི་རི་བོ།

dra mi nyen dang dra mi nyen gyi da   rin po cheyi ri wo
Uttaramantriṇa, Kurava and Kaurava, the mountain of jewels,

དཔག་བསམ་གྱི་ཤིང་། འདོད་འཇོའི་བ། མ་རྨོས་པའི་ལོ་ཏོག །

pak sam gyi shing   dö joyi ba   ma mö pa yi lo tok
the wish-fulfilling tree, the cow who fulfills wishes, the untilled crops,

འཁོར་ལོ་རིན་པོ་ཆེ། ནོར་བུ་རིན་པོ་ཆེ། བཙུན་མོ་རིན་པོ་ཆེ།

khor lo rin po che   nor bu rin po che   tsün mo rin po che
the precious wheel, the precious jewel, the precious queen, the precious

བློན་པོ་རིན་པོ་ཆེ། གླང་པོ་རིན་པོ་ཆེ། རྟ་མཆོག་རིན་པོ་ཆེ།

lön po rin po che   lang po rin po che   ta chok rin po che
minister, the precious elephant, the precious horse, the precious

དམག་དཔོན་རིན་པོ་ཆེ། གཏེར་ཆེན་པོའི་བུམ་པ།

mak pön rin po che   ter chen po yi bum pa
general, the vase of great treasure, the maiden of charm, the maiden

སྒེག་མོ་མ། ཕྲེང་བ་མ། གླུ་མ། གར་མ། མེ་ཏོག་མ།

gek mo ma   treng wa ma   lu ma   gar ma   me tok ma
of garlands, the maiden of song, the maiden of flowers, the maiden of

བདུག་སྤོས་མ། སྣང་གསལ་མ། དྲི་ཆབ་མ། ཉི་མ། ཟླ་བ།

duk pö ma   nang sal ma   dri chap ma   nyi ma   da wa
incense, the maiden of lamps, the maiden of perfume, the sun,

127

རིན་པོ་ཆེའི་གདུགས། ཕྱོགས་ལས་རྣམ་པར་རྒྱལ་བའི་རྒྱལ་མཚན།

rin po cheyi duk   chok le nam par gyal way gyal tsen
the moon, the jeweled parasol, the banner victorious in all directions,

དབུས་སུ་ལྷ་དང་མིའི་དཔལ་འབྱོར་ཕུན་སུམ་ཚོགས་པ་མ་ཚང་བ་མེད་པ།

ü su lha dang miyi pal jor pün sum tsok pa ma tsang wa me pa
and in the center all the resplendent wealth of gods and humans, none

རབ་འབྱམས་རྒྱ་མཚོའི་རྡུལ་གྱི་གྲངས་ལས་འདས་པ་མངོན་པར་བཀོད་དེ།

rap jam gya tsoy dül gyi drang le de pa ngön par kö pa de
left out, more numerous than the atoms in infinite oceans.

བླ་མ་ཡི་དམ་སངས་རྒྱས་བྱང་ཆུབ་སེམས་དཔའ་དཔའ་བོ་མཁའ་འགྲོ་ཆོས་

la ma yi dam sang gye jang chup sem pa pa wo khan dro chö
I offer this to the gurus, yidams, buddhas, bodhisattvas, heroes, dakinis,

སྐྱོང་སྲུང་མའི་ཚོགས་དང་བཅས་པ་རྣམས་ལ་དབུལ་བར་བགྱིའོ། །

kyong sung may tsok dang che pa nam la ul war gyi o
and gatherings of Dharma protectors.

ཐུགས་རྗེས་འགྲོ་བའི་དོན་དུ་བཞེས་སུ་གསོལ། །

tuk jey dro way dön du she su söl
I pray you accept this with compassion for the sake of beings.

བཞེས་ནས་བྱིན་གྱིས་བརླབ་ཏུ་གསོལ། ཞེས་དང་།

she ne jin gyi lap tu söl
I ask that you then grant your blessings.

ཕྱོགས་བཅུ་དུས་གསུམ་བཞུགས་པ་ཡི། །

chok chu dü sum shuk pa yi
To the buddhas and the bodhisattvas

སངས་རྒྱས་བྱང་ཆུབ་སེམས་དཔའ་དང་། །

sang gye jang chup sem pa dang
Who dwell in the three times and ten directions,

བླ་མ་རྡོ་རྗེ་སློབ་དཔོན་དང་། །

la ma dor je lop pön dang
As well as to the guru vajra masters

ཡི་དམ་ལྷ་ཚོགས་འཁོར་དང་བཅས། །

yi dam lha tsok khor dang che
And yidam deities with their retinues—

དུས་གསུམ་བདེ་གཤེགས་མ་ལུས་པ། །

dü sum de shek ma lü pa
To all the sugatas of the three times—

གླིང་བཞི་རི་རབ་བཅས་པ་དང་། །

ling shi ri rpa che pa dang
I gather in a single mandala

གླིང་བཞི་བྱེ་བ་ཕྲག་བརྒྱ་དང་། །

ling shi je wa trak gya dang
Mount Meru along with the four continents,

བྱེ་བ་འབུམ་དང་དུང་ཕྱུར་ཏེ། །

je wa bum dang dun chur te
A billion sets of the four continents,

མཚལ་གཅིག་ཏུ་བསྡུས་ནས་ནི། །

men del chik tu dü ne ni
A thousand billion and a million billion,

མོས་བློས་གོང་མ་རྣམས་ལ་འབུལ། །

chö lö gong ma nam la bül
And offer it to the great beings with longing.

ཐུགས་རྗེས་བརྩེར་དགོངས་བཞེས་སུ་གསོལ། །

tuk je tser gong she su söl
I pray you accept it with compassion,

བཞེས་ནས་བྱིན་གྱིས་བརླབ་ཏུ་གསོལ། །

she ne jin gyi lap tu söl
Once you've accepted it, please grant your blessings.

ཨོྃ་མཚལ་པཱུ་ཛ་མེ་གྷ་ས་མུ་ད་སྥ་ར་ཎ་ས་མ་ཡེ་ཨཱཿཧཱུྃ།

oṃ maṇḍala pūja megha samudra spharaṇa samaye āḥ hūṃ
OṂ MAṆḌALA PŪJA MEGHA SAMUDRA SPHARAṆA SAMAYE ĀḤ HŪṂ

མཉེས་བྱེད་མཚལ་བཟང་པོ་འདི་ཕུལ་བས། །

nye che men del sang po di pul way
By offering this fine and pleasing mandala,

བྱང་ཆུབ་ལམ་ལ་བར་ཆད་མི་འབྱུང་ཞིང་། །

jang chup lam la bar che mi jung shing
May there be no obstructions on the path of bodhi.

དུས་གསུམ་བདེ་གཤེགས་དགོངས་པ་རྟོགས་པ་དང་། །

dü sum de shek gong pa tok pa dang
May I realize the intent of the sugatas of the three times.

སྲིད་པར་མི་འཁྲུལ་ཞི་བར་མི་གནས་ཤིང་། །

si par mi trul shi war mi ne shing
Neither confused in existence nor dwelling in peace,

ནམ་མཁའ་མཉམ་པའི་འགྲོ་བ་སྒྲོལ་བར་ཤོག །

nam kha nyam pay dro wa dröl war shok
May I free all sentient beings throughout space.

མཎྜལ་སྒྲུབས་གསོག་པ་ཡིན་ན།

If accumulating mandala offerings:

ས་གཞི་སྤོས་ཆུས་བྱུགས་ཤིང་མེ་ཏོག་བཀྲམ། །

sa shi pö chü juk shing me tok tram
This earth, perfumed with scented water, strewn with flowers,

རི་རབ་གླིང་བཞི་ཉི་ཟླས་བརྒྱན་པ་འདི། །

ri rap ling shi nyi day gyen pa di
Graced with Mount Meru, the four lands, the sun and moon,

སངས་རྒྱས་ཞིང་དུ་དམིགས་ཏེ་ཕུལ་བ་ཡིས། །

sang gye shing du mik tu pül wa yi
I visualize to be a buddha realm and offer

འགྲོ་ཀུན་རྣམ་དག་ཞིང་ལ་སྤྱོད་པར་ཤོག །

dro kün nam dak shing la chö par shok
So that all beings enjoy a perfectly pure realm.

ཅེས་རྒྱས་བསྡུས་སྐབས་དང་སྦྱར་ཏེ།

Recite the long or short according to the occasion.

སྐུ་གསུམ་ཡོངས་རྫོགས་རྟ་བའི་ཚོགས་རྣམས་ལ། །

ku sum yong dzok la may tsok nam la

To the gatherings of gurus who have perfected the three kayas

ཕྱི་ནང་གསང་གསུམ་དེ་བཞིན་ཉིད་ཀྱིས་མཆོད། །

chi nang sang sum de shin nyi kyi chö

I make the outer, inner, secret, and suchness offerings.

བདག་ལུས་ལོངས་སྤྱོད་སྣང་སྲིད་ཡོངས་བཞེས་ལ། །

dak lü long chö nang si yong she la

Accept my body and wealth as well as all that appears and exists.

རྟ་མེད་མཆོག་གི་དངོས་གྲུབ་སྩལ་དུ་གསོལ། །

la me chok gi ngö drup tsal du söl

Bestow on me the unexcelled supreme accomplishment—

ཕྱག་རྒྱ་ཆེན་པོའི་དངོས་གྲུབ་སྩལ་དུ་གསོལ། །

chak gya chen poy ngö drup tsal du söl

Please grant the accomplishment of mahamudra.

ཕྱག་འཚལ་བ་དང་མཆོད་ཅིང་བཤགས་པ་དང་། །

chak tsal wa dang chö ching shak pa dang

I dedicate to enlightenment whatever

རྗེས་སུ་ཡི་རང་བསྐུལ་ཞིང་གསོལ་བ་ཡི། །

je su yi rang kul shing söl wa yin

Slight merit I have gathered from prostrating,

133

དགེ་བ་ཆུང་ཟད་བདག་གིས་ཅི་བསགས་པ། །

ge wa chung se dak gi chi sak pa
And offering, confessing, and rejoicing,

ཐམས་ཅད་བདག་གིས་བྱང་ཆུབ་ཕྱིར་བསྔོའོ། །

tam che dak gi jang chup chir ngo o
Requesting, and from making supplications.

བདག་གཞན་མཁའ་མཉམ་བདོག་པ་ཀུན་ཕུལ་ནས། །

dak shen kha nyam dok pa kün pul ne
By offering all my own possessions
And those of all others throughout space,

འགྲོ་ཀུན་ཚོགས་གཉིས་རབ་ཏུ་གང་གྱུར་ཏེ། །

dro kün tsok nyi rap tu gang gyur te
All wanderers fulfill completely
The two accumulations.

ཚོགས་ཞིང་འོད་ཞུ་བདག་དང་རོ་མཉམ་གྱུར།

tsok shing ö shu dak dang ro nyam gyur
The field of accumulations melts into light
And we become equal in taste.

Guru Yoga

༈ བྱིན་རླབས་མྱུར་དུ་འཇུག་པར་བྱེད་པའི་བླ་མའི་རྣལ་འབྱོར་ནི།

Guru yoga, which brings blessings swiftly:

ཁྱད་པར་དྭགས་པོ་བཀའ་བརྒྱུད་ཆོས་གྲུས་ཀྱི་བཀའ་བབ་ཡིན་པས་རྗེས་འཇུག་རྣམས་ཀྱང་བྱིན་
རླབས་འདི་ཆེ་བས་ཏེ་ཚོམ་མེད་པར་སེམས་རྩེ་གཅིག་པས།

*Since the Dakpo Kagyu in particular is a transmission of devotion, its
followers also should have no doubt that these blessings are great. With one-
pointed concentration:*

སྤྱི་བོར་པདྨ་ཉི་ཟླའི་གདན་སྟེང་དུ། །

chi wor pe ma nyi day den teng du
Above my crown on a lotus, sun, moon seat

རྩ་བའི་བླ་མ་རྡོ་རྗེ་འཆང་དབང་པོ། །

tsa way la ma dor je chang wang po
Is my root guru, mighty Vajradhara,

རྒྱན་ལྡན་རྡོར་དྲིལ་འཛིན་པའི་ཕྱག་རྒྱ་བསྣོལ། །

gyen den dor dril dzin pay chak gya nöl
Adorned and holding vajra and bell in his crossed hands.

རྡོ་རྗེ་གདན་བཞུགས་བརྒྱུད་པའི་བླ་མ་དང་། །

dor je den shuk gyü pay la ma dang
He sits on a vajra seat. The lineage gurus

དཀོན་མཆོག་རྒྱ་མཚོ་ཐོ་བརྩེགས་ཁྲོམ་དུ་ཚོགས། །

kön chok gya tso to tsek trom du tsok
And an ocean of Jewels gather in a column and a crowd.

ཨོཾ་ཁྱབ་བདག་དངོས་པོ་ཀུན་གྱི་རང་བཞིན་ཅན། །

oṃ kyap dak ngö po kün gyi rang shin chen
OṂ Pervasive lord, whose nature is of all things,

གནས་མེད་འགྲོ་འོང་བྲལ་བ་ནམ་མཁའ་བཞིན། །

ne me dro way dral wa nam kha shin
Like space, you do not stay or go or come.

གཤེགས་དང་འབྱོན་པའི་མཚན་མ་མི་མངའ་ཡང་། །

shek dang jön pay tsen ma mi nga yang
You have no marks of leaving or arriving.

ཆུ་ཟླ་བཞིན་དུ་གར་དམིགས་དེར་སྣང་བ། །

chu da shin du gar mik der nang wa
Like a moon in water, you appear where we look.

བདུད་དཔུང་འཇོམས་མཛད་དཔལ་ལྡན་ཧེ་རུ་ཀ །

dü pung jom dze pal den he ru ka
Glorious heruka who defeats the hordes of Mara,

བླ་མ་ཡི་དམ་མཁའ་འགྲོ་འཁོར་དང་བཅས། །

la ma yi dam khan dro khor dang che
Gurus, yidams, dakinis, and your retinues,

བདག་གི་དད་པས་དེང་འདིར་གསོལ་འདེབས་ན། །

dak gi de pay deng dir söl dep na
Now that I pray to you with faith, through the power

དམིགས་མེད་སྙིང་རྗེའི་དབང་གིས་འདིར་གསལ་མཛོད། །

mik me nying jey wang gi dir sal dzö
Of nonreferential compassion, make yourselves visible here.

འོག་མིན་ཆོས་ཀྱི་དབྱིངས་ཀྱི་པོ་བྲང་ནས། །

ok min chö kyi ying kyi po drang ne
In the dharma expanse palace of Akanishtha

དུས་གསུམ་སངས་རྒྱས་ཀུན་གྱི་ངོ་བོ་ཉིད། །

dü sum sang gye kün gyi ngo wo nyi
Is the essence of all buddhas of the three times,

རང་སེམས་ཆོས་སྐུར་མངོན་སུམ་སྟོན་མཛད་པ། །

rang sem chö kur ngön sum tön dze pa
Who shows me directly my mind is dharmakaya.

དཔལ་ལྡན་བླ་མ་དམ་པ་ལ་ཕྱག་འཚལ། །

pal den la ma dam pa la chak tsal
I prostrate to the glorious, exalted guru.

དངོས་དང་ལོངས་སྤྱོད་ཡིད་ཀྱིས་སྤྲུལ་པ་ཡི། །

ngö dang long chö yi kyi trul pa yi
I offer you everything—my body, wealth,

མཆོད་པ་ཀུན་གྱིས་མཆོད་ཅིང་བསྟོད་པར་བགྱི། །

chö pa kün gyi chö ching tö par gyi
And imagined offerings—and sing your praise.

སྔར་བྱས་སྡིག་པ་མ་ལུས་བཤགས་པར་བྱ། །

ngar che dik pa ma lü shak par ja
I confess every misdeed I have done;

སྡིག་པ་གཞན་ཡང་ལེན་ཆད་མི་བགྱིད་དོ། །

dik pa shen yang len che mi gyi do
I'll never do another one again.

འགྲོ་ཀུན་དགེ་བ་ཀུན་ལ་རྗེས་ཡི་རང༌། །

dro kün ge wa kün la je yi rang
I rejoice in all the virtues of all beings

བྱང་ཆུབ་མཆོག་གི་རྒྱུར་ནི་བསྔོ་བར་བགྱི། །

jang chup chok gi gyur ni ngo war gyi
And dedicate them as the cause of supreme bodhi.

མྱ་ངན་མི་འདའ་བཞུགས་པར་གསོལ་བ་འདེབས། །

nya ngen mi da shuk par söl wa dep
I pray you stay, not passing to nirvana,

ཐེག་མཆོག་བླ་མེད་ཆོས་འཁོར་བསྐོར་བར་བསྐུལ། །

tek chok la me chö khor kor war kül
And turn the wheel of the supreme, unexcelled vehicle.

བྱམས་དང་སྙིང་རྗེ་ཕྱོགས་མེད་འབྱངས་པ་དང་། །

jam dang nyin je chok me jang pa dang
Please grant your blessings that I may be fully trained

དོན་དམ་ལྷན་ཅིག་སྐྱེས་པའི་ཡེ་ཤེས་དེ། །

dön dam lhen chik kye pay ye she de
In loving-kindness and compassion without bias

རྒྱལ་བ་སྲས་བཅས་རྣམས་ཀྱི་རྟོགས་པ་ལྟར། །

gyal wa se che nam kyi tok pa tar
And that I realize ultimate, coemergent wisdom

བདག་གིས་མངོན་སུམ་རྟོགས་པར་བྱིན་གྱིས་རློབས། །

dak gi ngö sum tok par jin gyi lop
Directly, just as have the victors and their children.

སྒྱུ་ལུས་སྤྲུལ་སྐུར་རྟོགས་པར་བྱིན་གྱིས་རློབས། །

gyu lü trul kur tok pa jin gyi lop
Bless me to realize the illusory body is nirmanakaya.

སྲོག་རྩོལ་ལོངས་སྐུར་རྟོགས་པར་བྱིན་གྱིས་རློབས། །

sok tsol long kur tok pa jin gyi lop
Bless me to realize that life force is sambhogakaya.

རང་སེམས་ཆོས་སྐུར་རྟོགས་པར་བྱིན་གྱིས་རློབས། །

rang sem chö kur tok pa jin gyi lop
Bless me to realize my own mind is dharmakaya.

སྐུ་གསུམ་དབྱེར་མེད་འཆར་བར་བྱིན་གྱིས་རློབས། །

ku sum yer me char war jin gyi lop

Bless me that the three kayas arise inseparably.

དེ་ནས་ཕྱག་ཆེན་བརྒྱུད་པའི་བླ་མ་ལ་གསོལ་འདེབས་ཏེ།

Next is the supplication to the gurus of the lineage of mahamudra:

དངོས་ཀུན་ཁྱབ་བདག་དཔལ་ལྡན་རྡོ་རྗེ་འཆང་། །

ngö kün khyap dak pal den dor je chang

Pervasive lord of all things, glorious Vajradhara,

ས་བཅུའི་དབང་ཕྱུག་བློ་གྲོས་རིན་ཆེན་ཞབས། །

sa chuy wang chuk lo drö rin chen shap

Master of the tenth level, Lodrö Rinchen,

འཕགས་ཡུལ་གྲུབ་པའི་གཙོ་བོ་ས་ར་ཧ། །

pak yül drup pay tso wo sa ra ha

And Saraha, foremost siddha of the Noble Land:

གསོལ་བ་འདེབས་སོ་ལྷན་སྐྱེས་ཡེ་ཤེས་སྩོལ། །

söl wa dep so lhen kye ye she tsöl

I pray to you; grant me coemergent wisdom.

ཆོས་ཉིད་དོན་གཟིགས་འཕགས་པ་ཀླུ་སྒྲུབ་དང་། །

chö nyi dön sik pak pa lu drup dang

Noble Nagarjuna who sees the dharmata,

ཕྱག་རྒྱ་ཆེ་བརྙེས་དཔལ་ལྡན་ཤ་བ་རི། །

cha gya che nye pal den sha wa ri
Glorious Shawari who achieved mahamudra,

སྙིང་པོའི་དོན་གཟིགས་རྗེ་བོ་མཻ་ཏྲི་པ། །

nying po dön sik jo wo mai tri pa
Lord Maitripa who saw the meaning of the essence:

གསོལ་བ་འདེབས་སོ་ལྷན་སྐྱེས་ཡེ་ཤེས་སྩོལ། །

söl wa dep so lhen kye ye she tsöl
I pray to you; grant me coemergent wisdom.

མར་པ་མི་ལ་རྗེ་བཙུན་སྒམ་པོ་པ། །

mar pa mi la je tsün gam po pa
Marpa, Milarepa, venerable Gampopa,

དུས་གསུམ་མཁྱེན་པ་རས་ཆེན་སྤོམ་བྲག་པ། །

dü sum khyen pa re chen pom drak pa
Dusum Khyenpa, Rechen Pomdrakpa,

གཀྲ་པ་དང་མཁས་གྲུབ་ཨོ་རྒྱན་པ། །

kar ma pa dang khe drup or gyen pa
Karma Pakshi, scholar and siddhi Orgyenpa:

གསོལ་བ་འདེབས་སོ་ལྷན་སྐྱེས་ཡེ་ཤེས་སྩོལ། །

söl wa dep so lhen kye ye she tsöl
I pray to you; grant me coemergent wisdom.

རང་བྱུང་རྡོ་རྗེ་རྒྱལ་བ་གཡུང་སྟོན་པ། །

rang jung dor je gyal wa yung tön pa
Rangjung Dorje, Gyalwa Yungtönpa,

རོལ་པའི་རྡོ་རྗེ་རྟོགས་ལྡན་མཁའ་སྤྱོད་དབང་། །

röl pay dor je tok den kha chö wang
Rolpay Dorje, realized Khachö Wangpo,

དེ་བཞིན་གཤེགས་པ་རཏྣ་བྷ་དྲ་ལ། །

de shin shek pa rat na bha dra la
Deshin Shekpa, and Ratnabhadra:

གསོལ་བ་འདེབས་སོ་ལྷན་སྐྱེས་ཡེ་ཤེས་སྩོལ། །

söl wa dep so lhen kye ye she tsöl
I pray to you; grant me coemergent wisdom.

མཐོང་བ་དོན་ལྡན་ཀུན་མཁྱེན་འཇམ་དཔལ་བཟང་། །

tong wa dön den kün khyen jam pal sang
Tongwa Dönden, all knowing Jampal Sangpo,

དཔལ་འབྱོར་དོན་གྲུབ་ཆོས་གྲགས་རྒྱ་མཚོ་དང་། །

pal jor dön drup chö drak gya tso dang
Paljor Döndrup, Chödrak Gyatso,

བཀྲ་ཤིས་དཔལ་འབྱོར་མི་བསྐྱོད་རྡོ་རྗེ་ལ། །

ta shi pal jor mi kyö dor je la
Tashi Paljor, and Mikyö Dorje:

གསོལ་བ་འདེབས་སོ་ལྷུན་སྐྱེས་ཡེ་ཤེས་སྩོལ། །

söl wa dep so lhen kye ye she tsöl
I pray to you; grant me coemergent wisdom.

དཀོན་མཆོག་ཡན་ལག་དབང་ཕྱུག་རྡོ་རྗེ་འཛིན། །

kön chok yen lak wang chuk dor je dzin
Könchok Yenlak, Wangchuk Dorje,

ཆོས་ཀྱི་དབང་ཕྱུག་ཆོས་དབྱིངས་རྡོ་རྗེ་མཆོག །

chö kyi wang chuk chö ying dor je chok
Chökyi Wangchuk, great Chöying Dorje,

ཡེ་ཤེས་སྙིང་པོ་ཡེ་ཤེས་རྡོ་རྗེ་ལ། །

ye she nying po ye she dor je la
Yeshe Nyingpo, and Yeshe Dorje:

གསོལ་བ་འདེབས་སོ་ལྷུན་སྐྱེས་ཡེ་ཤེས་སྩོལ། །

söl wa dep so lhen kye ye she tsöl
I pray to you; grant me coemergent wisdom.

ཆོས་ཀྱི་དོན་གྲུབ་བྱང་ཆུབ་རྡོ་རྗེ་དང་། །

chö kyi dön drup jang chup dor je dang
Chökyi Döndrup, Jangchup Dorje,

བསྟན་པའི་ཉིན་བྱེད་བདུད་ཚོགས་འདུལ་རྡོ་རྗེ། །

ten pay nyin che dü tsok dül dor je
Tenpay Nyinche, Düdul Dorje,

ཚོས་གྲུབ་རྒྱ་མཚོ་པད་མ་ཉིན་བྱེད་ལ། །

chö drup gya tso pe ma nyin che la
Chödrup Gyatso, and Pema Nyinche:

གསོལ་བ་འདེབས་སོ་ལྷན་སྐྱེས་ཡེ་ཤེས་སྩོལ། །

söl wa dep so lhen kye ye she tsöl
I pray to you; grant me coemergent wisdom.

ཐེག་མཆོག་རྡོ་རྗེ་བློ་གྲོས་མཐའ་ཡས་དང་། །

tek chok dor je lo drö ta ye dang
Tekchok Dorje, Lodrö Taye,

མཁའ་ཁྱབ་རྡོ་རྗེ་པད་མ་དབང་མཆོག་ཞབས། །

kha khyap dor je pe ma wang chok shap
Khakhyap Dorje, Pema Wangchuk,

མཁྱེན་བརྩེ་འོད་ཟེར་རིག་པའི་རྡོ་རྗེ་ལ། །

khyen tse ö ser rik pay dor je la
Khyentse Öser, and Rikpe Dorje:

གསོལ་བ་འདེབས་སོ་ལྷན་སྐྱེས་ཡེ་ཤེས་སྩོལ། །

söl wa dep so lhen kye ye she tsöl
I pray to you; grant me coemergent wisdom.

འདིའི་མ་དཔེར་དྲུང་བཞི་པ་མ་ཚང་བས་ཁ་སྐོང་དང་། ཚོས་གྲུབ་རྒྱ་མཚོ་མན་ཆད་ཀྱི་ཞལ་སློང་རྒྱལ་དབང་བཅུ་བདུན་པས་མཛད།

The Seventeenth Karmapa added the fourth Karmapa, who was missing in the manuscript, and all the masters from Chödrup Gyatso on down.

གཞི་ལམ་འབྲས་བུའི་གནས་ལུགས་ཕྱག་རྒྱ་ཆེ། །

shi lam dre buy ne luk chak gya che
You are so kind to point out my genuine face,

གཉུག་མའི་རང་ངོ་སྟོན་མཛད་བཀའ་དྲིན་ཅན། །

nyuk may rang ngo trö dze ka drin chen
Mahamudra, the nature of ground, path, and result.

སངས་རྒྱས་ཀུན་འདུས་རྩ་བའི་བླ་མ་ལ། །

sang gye kün dü tsa way la ma la
You are all the buddhas in person, root guru:

གསོལ་བ་འདེབས་སོ་ལྷན་སྐྱེས་ཡེ་ཤེས་སྩོལ། །

söl wa dep so lhen kye ye she tsöl
I pray to you; grant me coemergent wisdom.

དངོས་གྲུབ་གཉིས་སྩོལ་ཡི་དམ་ལྷ་ཚོགས་དང་། །

ngö drup nyi tsöl yi dam lha tsok dang
Gatherings of yidams who grant the two siddhis,

ཕྲིན་ལས་ཀུན་བདག་ཆོས་སྐྱོང་སྲུང་མའི་ཚོགས། །

trin le kün dak chö kyong sung may tsok
Dharma protectors, masters of activity,

བཀའ་སྡོད་དམ་ཅན་རྒྱ་མཚོའི་ཚོགས་བཅས་ལ། །

ka dö dam chen gya tsoy tsok che la
And the ocean of samaya-bound who take commands:

གསོལ་བ་འདེབས་སོ་ལྷུན་སྐྱེས་ཡེ་ཤེས་སྩོལ། །

söl wa dep so lhen kye ye she tsöl
I pray to you; grant me coemergent wisdom.

དེ་ལྟར་གསོལ་བ་བཏབ་པའི་བྱིན་རླབས་ཀྱིས། །

de tar söl wa tap pay jin lap kyi
Due to the blessings of praying thus, may I realize

འཁོར་འདས་དངོས་ཀུན་བསལ་བཞག་སྤང་བླང་དང་། །

khor de ngö kun sal shak pang lang dang
The ground of all, free of samsara and nirvana,

ཡོད་མེད་ལ་སོགས་ཀུན་བྲལ་ཀུན་གྱི་གཞི། །

yö me la sok kün dral kün gyi shi
Of all things, adding, removing, shunning, and taking,

གནས་ལུགས་གཞི་ཡི་ཕྱག་རྒྱ་ཆེ་རྟོགས་ཤོག །

ne luk shi yi chak gya che tok shok
Being and not being—the nature, ground mahamudra.

རྟོགས་བྱ་རྟོགས་བྱེད་རྟོགས་པ་མ་དམིགས་ཤིང་། །

tok ja tok che tok pa ma mik shing
Not seeing the realized, realizer, or realization;

བསྒྲིབ་བྱ་སྒྲིབ་བྱེད་སྒྲིབ་པ་སྤང་མེད་པར། །

drip ja drip che drip pa pang me par
Not giving up the obscured, obscurer, and obscuration,

བསྒྲོད་བྱ་བསྒྲོད་བྱེད་ལམ་ལས་རབ་འདས་པའི། །

drö ja dö che lam le rap de pay
May I transcend the path, destination, and goer

ལམ་གྱི་ཕྱག་རྒྱ་ཆེན་པོ་མངོན་གྱུར་ཤོག །

lam gyi chak gya chen po ngön gyur shok
And manifest the mahamudra of the path.

ཐོབ་བྱ་ཐོབ་བྱེད་ཐོབ་པ་མ་དམིགས་ཤིང་། །

top ja top che top pa ma mik shing
The achieved, achiever, and achievement are not seen.

སྤང་ཐོབ་གཉིས་མེད་གཞི་འབྲས་དབྱེར་མེད་པ། །

pang top nyi me shi dre er me pa
Abandonment and achievement are not two; ground and result

དངོས་བྲལ་དངོས་པོ་ཀུན་གྱི་རང་བཞིན་ཅན། །

ngö dral ngö po kün gyi rang shin chen
Inseparable. Devoid of things, its nature is of all things.

འབྲས་བུའི་ཕྱག་རྒྱ་ཆེན་པོ་མངོན་གྱུར་ཤོག །

dre buy chak gya chen po ngön gyur shok
May I manifest the mahamudra of the result.

སྐབས་འདིར།
At this point:

147

མ་ནམ་མཁའ་དང་མཉམ་པའི་སེམས་ཅན་ཐམས་ཅད་བླ་མ་སངས་རྒྱས་རིན་པོ་

ma nam kha dang nyam pay sem chen tam che la ma sang gye rin

My mothers, all beings throughout space, go for refuge to the guru,

ཆེ་ལ་སྐྱབས་སུ་མཆིའོ། །དེ་བཞིན་དུ།

po che la kyap sum chi o

the precious buddha.

མ་ནམ་མཁའ་དང་མཉམ་པའི་སེམས་ཅན་ཐམས་ཅད་ཀུན་ཁྱབ་ཆོས་ཀྱི་སྐུ་ལ་

ma nam kha dang nyam pay sem chen tam che kun khyap chö kyi ku

My mothers, all beings throughout space, go for refuge to the guru,

སྐྱབས་སུ་མཆིའོ། །

la kyap sum chi o

the pervasive dharmakaya.

མ་ནམ་མཁའ་དང་མཉམ་པའི་སེམས་ཅན་ཐམས་ཅད་བླ་མ་བདེ་ཆེན་ལོངས་སྤྱོད་

ma nam kha dang nyam pay sem chen tam che la ma de chen long

My mothers, all beings throughout space, go for refuge to the guru,

རྫོགས་པའི་སྐུ་ལ་སྐྱབས་སུ་མཆིའོ། །

chö dzok pay ku la kyap sum chi o

the great bliss sambhogakaya.

མ་རྣམ་མཁའ་དང་མཉམ་པའི་སེམས་ཅན་ཐམས་ཅད་བླ་མ་ཐུགས་རྗེ་སྤྲུལ་པའི་སྐུ་

ma nam kha dang nyam pay sem chen tam che la ma tuk je trul pay
My mothers, all beings throughout space, go for refuge to the guru,

ལ་སྐྱབས་སུ་མཆིའོ། །ཞེས་མ་རྣམས་པའི་སྐོར་གྱི་བསྟེན་པའམ།

ku la kyap sum chi o
the compassionate nirmanakaya.

གཙོ་བ་མཐེན། །སོགས་བྱའོ། །

karmapa khyenno
Or recite: KARMAPA KHYENNO *and so forth.*

149

ཡང་ན། བླ་མ་རིན་པོ་ཆེ་ལ་གསོལ་བ་འདེབས། །

la ma rin po che la söl wa dep
Alternatively: I pray and supplicate my precious guru.

བདག་འཛིན་བློ་ཡིས་གཏོང་བར་བྱིན་གྱིས་རློབས། །

dak dzin lo yi tong par jin gyi lop
Bless me to give up clinging to an ego.

དགོས་མེད་རྒྱུད་ལ་སྐྱེ་བར་བྱིན་གྱིས་རློབས། །

gö me gyü la kye war jin gyi lop
Bless me to realize that I have no needs.

རང་སེམས་སྐྱེ་མེད་རྟོགས་པར་བྱིན་གྱིས་རློབས། །

rang sem kye me tok par jin gyi lop
Bless me to realize that my mind is unborn.

འཁྲུལ་པ་རང་སར་ཞི་བར་བྱིན་གྱིས་རློབས། །

trul pa rang sar shi war jin gyi lop
Bless me that confusion naturally subside.

སྣང་ཞིང་ཆོས་སྐུར་རྟོགས་པར་བྱིན་གྱིས་རློབས། །

nang shi chö kur tok par jin gyi lop
Bless me to realize everything is dharmakaya.

མཐར་བླ་མ་རྒྱང་འབོད་དྲག་དྲག་ལ་ཡུན་རིང་དུ་སྐྱང་བ་འགྱུར་ངེས་སུ་ཉུ།

At the end, call the guru from afar intensely and for a long time, and rest until your perceptions definitely transform.

ब्ल་མ་དམ་པ་བདག་ལ་དབང་བཞི་རྫོགས་པར་བསྐུར་དུ་གསོལ།

la ma dam pa dak la wang shi dzok par kur du söl
Exalted guru, I pray you grant me the four complete empowerments.

རྩེ་གཅིག་གུས་པའི་དད་པ་ཕུལ་བ་ལས། །

tse chik gü pay de pa pul wa le
From offering this faith that is whole-hearted longing,

འཁོར་རྣམས་འོད་དུ་ཞུ་ནས་བླ་མར་ཐིམ། །

khor nam ö du shu ne la mar tim
The retinue melts into light and then dissolves

དེ་ཡང་འོད་ཞུ་བདག་ལ་ཐིམ་པ་ལས། །

de yang ö shu dak la tim pa le
Into the guru, who melts into me. His body

སྐུ་དང་བདག་ལུས་འདྲེས་པས་བུམ་དབང་ཐོབ། །

ku dang dak lü dre pay bum wang top
Mixing with mine, I receive the vase empowerment.

དེ་བཞིན་གསུང་དང་ཐུགས་དང་ཡེ་ཤེས་ནི། །

de shin sung dang tuk dang ye she ni
Likewise his speech and mind and wisdom mix

བདག་གི་ངག་ཡིད་ཡེ་ཤེས་དང་འདྲེས་པས། །

dak gi ngak yi ye she dang dre pay
With my speech, mind, and wisdom, so I receive

གསང་བ་ཤེས་རབ་ཡེ་ཤེས་བཞི་པའི་དབང་། །

sang wa she rap ye she shi pay wang

The secret, prajna wisdom, and fourth empowerments.

ཐོབ་ཅིང་སྒོ་གསུམ་དྲི་མ་དག་པར་སྦྱངས། །

top chink go sum dri ma dak par jang

The stains of my three gates are cleansed and purified,

སྐུ་བཞིའི་ས་བོན་རྒྱུད་ལ་བཞག་པར་མཛོད། །

ku shiyi sa bön gyü la shak par dzö

The seeds of the four kayas are planted in my being.

ཅེས་ཐུན་མཆམས་ཐམས་ཅད་དུ་མཉམ་གཞག་དང་དགེ་བ་བསྔོ་བར་བྱའོ། །དེ་ལྟར་ཐུན་མོང་མ་ཡིན་པའི་སྔོན་འགྲོ་བཞིའོ། །ཤུཏྪཔུཥྚཾ་རྐྲ་སྩུ།། །།

In all the breaks, dedicate the equipoise and the virtue. Those were the four uncommon preliminaries. ŚHUBHAPUṢHṬAṂ BHAVANTU

དཔལ་ལྡན་བླ་མ་དམ་པ་ཁྱེན་རྣམས་ཀྱིས། །

pal den la ma dam pa khyen nam kyi

Glorious exalted gurus, I ask that you

བདག་ལ་སྨིན་བྱེད་དབང་བཞི་བསྐུར་དུ་གསོལ། །

dak la min che wang shi kur du söl

Grant me the four empowerments that ripen.

རྒྱུད་བཞི་མྱུར་དུ་སྨིན་པར་བྱིན་གྱིས་རློབས། །

gyü shi nyur du min par jin gyi lop

Bless me to ripen my four streams of being.

ཕྲིན་ལས་རྣམ་བཞིའི་དངོས་གྲུབ་སྩལ་དུ་གསོལ། །

trin le nam shiy ngö drup tsal du söl

Please grant the siddhi of the four activities.

ཞེས་པའི་གསོལ་བ་བཏབ་པའི་མོད་ཉིད་ལ། །

she pay söl wa tap pay mö nyi la

The instant that I make this prayer, the retinue

འཁོར་རྣམས་འོད་ཞུ་གཙོ་བོའི་སྐུ་ལ་ཐིམ། །

khor nam ö shu tso woy ku la tim

Melts into light, dissolves into the principal,

གཙོ་བོ་དཀོན་མཆོག་ཀུན་འདུས་བདག་ཉིད་ལ། །

tso wo kön chok kün dü dak nyi la

The very embodiment of all the Jewels

རྣམ་པ་བླ་མ་དངོས་སུ་གསལ་གྱུར་པའི། །

nam pa la ma ngö su sal gyur pay
Actually visible in the guru's form.

མཛོད་སྤུའི་གནས་ནས་འོད་ཟེར་དཀར་པོ་འཕྲོས། །

dzö puy ne ne ö ser kar po trö
White light that shines forth from his brow dissolves into my forehead,

རང་གི་དཔྲལ་བར་ཐིམ་པས་ལུས་སྒྲིབ་དག །

rang gi tral war tim pay lü drip dak
Thus purifying the obscurations of body. I receive

བུམ་པའི་དབང་ཐོབ་བསྐྱེད་རིམ་བསྒོམ་ལ་དབང་། །

bum pay wang top kye rim gom la wang
The vase empowerment to practice the creation stage

འབྲས་བུ་སྤྲུལ་སྐུ་འགྲུབ་པའི་སྐལ་ལྡན་གྱུར། །

dre bu trul ku drup pay kal den gyur
And have the fortune to achieve the result, nirmanakaya.

མགྲིན་པའི་གནས་ནས་འོད་ཟེར་དམར་པོ་འཕྲོས། །

drin pay ne ne ö ser mar po trö
Red light that shines forth from his throat dissolves into my throat,

རང་གི་མགྲིན་པར་ཐིམ་པས་ངག་སྒྲིབ་དག །

rang gi drin par tim pay ngak drip dak
Thus purifying the obscurations of speech. I receive

གསང་བའི་དབང་ཐོབ་རྩ་རླུང་བསྒོམ་ལ་དབང་། །

sang way wang top tsa lung gom la wang

The secret empowerment to meditate on channels and winds

ལོངས་སྤྱོད་རྫོགས་སྐུ་འགྲུབ་པའི་སྐལ་ལྡན་གྱུར། །

long chö dzok ku drup pay kal den gyur

And have the fortune to achieve the result, sambhogakaya.

ཐུགས་ཀའི་གནས་ནས་འོད་ཟེར་སྔོན་པོ་འཕྲོས། །

tuk kay ne ne ö ser ngö po trö

Blue light that shines forth from his heart dissolves into my heart,

རང་གི་སྙིང་གར་ཐིམ་པས་ཡིད་སྒྲིབ་དག །

rang gi nying gar tim pay yi drip dak

Thus purifying the obscurations of mind. I receive

ཤེར་དབང་ཐོབ་ཅིང་སྙོམས་འཇུག་བསྒོམ་ལ་དབང་། །

sher wang top ching nyom juk gom la wang

The wisdom empowerment to meditate on the absorption

འབྲས་བུ་ཆོས་སྐུ་འགྲུབ་པའི་སྐལ་ལྡན་གྱུར། །

dre bu chö ku drup pay kal den gyur

And have the fortune to achieve the result, the dharmakaya.

གནས་གསུམ་འོད་ཟེར་དཀར་དམར་མཐིང་གསུམ་འཕྲོས། །

ne sum ö ser kar mar ting sum trö

White, red, and blue light from his three places shines to my three places

155

གནས་གསུམ་ལ་ཐིམ་སྒོ་གསུམ་དྲི་མ་དག །

ne sum la tim go sum dri ma dak

Thus purifying my three gates' obscurations. I receive

བཞི་པའི་དབང་ཐོབ་ཕྱག་ཆེན་བསྒོམ་ལ་དབང༌། །

shi pay wang top chak chen gom la wang

The fourth empowerment to meditate on mahamudra

ངོ་བོ་ཉིད་སྐུ་འགྲུབ་པའི་སྐལ་ལྡན་གྱུར། །

ngo wo nyi ku drup pay kal den gyur

And have the fortune to achieve the result, the essence kaya.

དེ་ནས་བླ་མ་འོད་ཞུ་རང་ལ་ཐིམ། །

de ne la ma ö shu rang la tim

The guru, melting into light, dissolves in me.

རང་གི་ལུས་ངག་ཡིད་གསུམ་བླ་མ་ཡི། །

rang gi lü ngak yi sum la ma yi

My body, speech, and mind become inseparable

རྡོ་རྗེ་གསུམ་པོ་དབྱེར་མེད་རོ་གཅིག་ཅིང༌། །

dor je sum po yer me ro chik ching

From the three vajras of the guru, one in taste:

Body as kaya, speech as mantra, mind as wisdom—

ཁྱེར་སོ་གསུམ་ལྡན་ལྷུན་གྲུབ་རང་གྲོལ་ལོ། །

khyer so sum den lhün drup rang dröl lo
The natural, spontaneously present liberation.

ཅེས་ཕྱུན་མོང་མ་ཡིན་པའི་སྔོན་འགྲོ་བཞིའི་རིམ་པའོ།།

Those were the stages of the four uncommon preliminaries.

མཐག་བསྔོ་བ་སྨོན་ལམ་དང་། བདེན་པ་བརྗོད་པ་ནི།

The dedications, aspirations, declaration of truth:

དགེ་འདིས་འགྲོ་བ་མ་ལུས་རྡོ་རྗེ་སེམས། །

ge diy dro wa ma lü dor je sem
I dedicate this virtue so all beings may attain

ཐབ་བདེའི་ཐབས་ཤེས་སྦྱོར་བས་འཆི་མེད་ཀྱི། །

tak dey tap she jor way chi me kyi
The Vajra Mind, eternal bliss that through the union of

ནང་གི་ལམ་ནས་རྡོ་རྗེར་འགྲོ་བ་ཡིས། །

nang gi lam ne dor jer dro wa yi
Prajna and means goes via the inner path of deathlessness

སངས་རྒྱས་ཉིད་ཀྱི་གོ་འཕང་ཐོབ་ཕྱིར་བསྔོ། །

sang gye nyi kyi go pang top chir ngo
To the Vajra and thus to the state of buddhahood itself.

དགེ་བ་འདི་ཡིས་མྱུར་དུ་བདག །

ge wa di yi nyur du dak
By this merit, may I swiftly

དཔལ་ལྡན་བླ་མ་འགྲུབ་གྱུར་ནས། །

pal den la ma drup gyur ne
Achieve the state of mahamudra.

འགྲོ་བ་གཅིག་ཀྱང་མ་ལུས་པ། །

dro wa chik kyang ma lü pa
May I then bring all sentient beings—

དེ་ཡི་ས་ལ་འགོད་པར་ཤོག །

de yi sa la gö par shok
Not one left out—into that state.

སངས་རྒྱས་སྐུ་གསུམ་བརྙེས་པའི་བྱིན་རླབས་དང་། །

sang gye ku sum nye pay jin lap dang
By the blessings of the Buddha gaining the three kayas,

ཆོས་ཉིད་མི་འགྱུར་བདེན་པའི་བྱིན་རླབས་དང་། །

chö nyi min gyur den pay jin lap dang
The blessings of the unchanging truth of the dharma nature,

དགེ་འདུན་མི་ཕྱེད་འདུན་པའི་བྱིན་རླབས་ཀྱིས། །

gen dün mi che dün pay jin lap kyi
And the blessings of the undivided intentions of the Sangha,

ཇི་ལྟར་སྨོན་ལམ་བཏབ་བཞིན་འགྲུབ་པར་ཤོག །

ji tar mön lam tap shin drup par shok

May my aspirations and dedications be fulfilled just so!

དེ་ལྟ་བུའི་ཆུལ་གྱིས་རྒྱུན་ཁྱེར་སྨོན་འགྲོའི་ཆོས་རྣམས་སྤྱོམ་ཆིག་ཙམ་དུ་ཡོངས་སུ་རྫོགས་པར་འགྱུར་
བ་སྟེ། ཆོས་སྨོར་ཞུགས་པའི་ལས་དང་པོ་པ་རྣམས་ལ་ཉེ་བར་མཁོ་བས་རྗེས་སུ་ཡི་རངས་བར་
མཛོད་ཅིག། །།

In this manner, the daily practice of the preliminaries are completed as a mere summary. It is necessary for beginners who have entered the gate of Dharma, so rejoice!

Notes

1. A central country in terms of the Dharma is one where there are all four branches of the fourfold community of bhikshus, bhikshunis, male lay practitioners who hold the five precepts, and female lay practitioners who hold the five precepts.

2. Since stars are not visible in the daytime, this is often used as an analogy for extreme rarity.

3. The channels being severed refers to the process of the inner channels ceasing to function at the time of death.

4. Rituals, totems, and charms from the Bön tradition that are used to ward off harm, illness, and death.

5. Literally, "Know me, lama." It is often said as an exclamation.

6. One of the four yogas of mahamudra practice, in which the equal nature of phenomena is realized.

7. The three poisons are delusion, desire, and hatred.

8. Speaking purposefully is missing from the original.

9. Especially in premodern times, a woman's life was so much more difficult than a man's that it was considered desirable to be reborn male.

10. The virtues that lead to merit refers to virtuous actions that will lead to a pleasant rebirth in samsara. The virtues that lead to liberation are the path of accumulation—the virtues that will develop into liberation.

11. That is, buckwheat seeds only grow buckwheat, and barley seeds only grow barley. Buckwheat seeds can never grow barley, and vice versa.

12. That is, this is the basic principle to keep in mind when considering your actions and their results.

13. In the realm of the Four Great Kings (the lowest of the god realms in the Desire realm), each day equals 50 human years. The day-length doubles in

each successively higher realm—100 years in the Thirty-Three, 200 in Conflict Free, and so forth, up to 1600 human years in Enjoying Others' Emanations.

14. That is, working night and day.

15. The five aggregates of grasping are the five aggregates of form, feeling, conception, formations, and consciousness. *Grasping* here refers to the afflictions, meaning that the aggregates are created because of the afflictions and are also the basis on which the afflictions arise.

16. The right arm is outside the left.

17. The thirteen peaceful ornaments consist of eight pieces of jewelry and five articles of clothing that adorn all samboghakaya forms: a crown representing the five Buddha families, earrings, a short necklace, armlets, long necklaces, bracelets, rings, anklets, a headband, a silk robe, an upper garment, a long white scarf, a belt and a lower garment.

18. A cross-legged posture in which each foot rests upturned on the opposite thigh.

19. The 32 marks and 80 signs are physical qualities of a great being such as a buddha. These include having golden skin, forty even teeth, an arm span equal to their height, and so forth.

20. The practice nowadays is to visualize the lamas starting with Rangjung Rigpe Dorje, Jamgön Khyentse Öser, Pema Wangchuk Gyalpo, Khakhyap Dorje, Jamgön Kongtrul Lodrö Thaye, and then from Pema Nyinche Wangpo as described in the text.

21. Six great Indian scholars: Nagarjuna, Aryadeva, Asanga, Vasubandhu, Dignaga, and Dharmakirti. if add the at begin. will not be spacey

22. The twelve types of scripture are the sutras, hymns of praise, prophecies, teachings in verse, aphorisms, narratives, biographies, histories, tales of previous births, extensive teachings, accounts of marvels, and teachings in profound doctrines.

23. The three lords of the families are Avalokiteshvara, Manjushri, and Vajrapani. The remaining five of the eight close sons are Maitreya, Kshitigarbha, Akashagarbha, Samantabhadra, and Nivaranvishkambin. The excellent pair refers to Shariputra and Maudgalyayana, two of Shakyamuni Buddha's foremost disciples. Ananda was a nephew of Shakyamuni Buddha who became his attendant and remembered every word the Buddha spoke. The sixteen arhats are the elders who promised to preserve the Buddha's

teachings. It is said they remain in various locations throughout the world until the regent Maitreya appears as a Buddha.

24. The five certainties are the certainty of place, which is always dwelling in the pure lands; certainty of body, which is having the marks and signs of a buddha; certainty of time, which means always; certainty of the teachings, which means always teaching the Mahayana; and certainty of retinue, which means a retinue of bodhisattvas. Created nirmanakayas are when a Buddha manifests as a thing such as a bridge to help beings. Incarnate nirmanakayas are buddhas who take birth, and supreme nirmanakayas are buddhas with the thirty-two marks and eighty signs who appear in impure realms.

25. That is, three times every day and three times every night.

26. Six texts used by the Kadampa school to train practitioners in meditation. These include the *Jataka Tales* and *Udanavarga* as texts about faith; *The Bodhisattva Levels* by Asanga and *Ornament of Clear Realization* by Maitreya as texts about samadhi; and *The Way of the Bodhisattva* and *The Compendium of Trainings*, both by Shantideva, as texts about conduct.

27. Shantideva, *The Way of the Bodhisattva*, Chapter 5, verse 100.

28. Walking, pacing, lying down, and sitting are the four different types of physical postures or activity the Buddha recommended for his monks. (Pacing refers to the walking meditation of pacing back and forth.) By extension, these four are taken to include everything one might do with their body.

29. Skt. *Trisamaya Vyūha rāja tantra*, Tib. *Dam tshig gsum bkod pa'i rgyal po zhes bya ba'i rgyud*.

30. Skt. *Abhidhana Uttara Tantra*, Tib. *mNgon par brjod pa'i rgyud bla ma*.

31. An OṂ (ཨོཾ) at the forehead, ĀḤ (ཨཱཿ) at the throat, and HŪṂ (ཧཱུྃ) at the heart.

32. From *The Sutra Requested by Caryamati* ('Phags pa spyod pa'i blo gros kyis zhus pa' mdo).

33. Murdering your father, murdering your mother, murdering an arhat, drawing blood from a buddha with malicious intent, and causing a schism in the Sangha. According to *The Treasury of Abhidharma*, the five near heinous deeds are raping your mother who is an arhat, killing a bodhisattva certain to awaken, killing a Noble learner, robbing the Sangha's food, and destroying a stupa. The four weighty actions are four sets of four negative actions of regression, criticism, errors, and denial. There are two explanations of the eightperversions. The first, from the sutra tradition, is wrong view, wrong thought, wrong speech, wrong action, wrong livelihood, wrong effort, wrong mindfulness, and wrong samadhi. The second set, which is from the

Nyingma tradition, is criticizing virtue, praising misdeeds, disturbing the virtuous, breaking up gatherings of the faithful, rejecting the guru, rejecting the yidam, rejecting one's siblings, and destroying powerful mandalas.

34. A causally compatible result is a result that is similar to its cause. For example, enjoying killing things can be a causally compatible result of killing in a previous life.

35. From *The Ritual of the Hundred Syllables* (*Yi ge brgya pa'i cho ga*), Dergye Tengyur rGyud 'grel ku pa, p. 295b.

36. OM VAJRA AMRITA KUNDALI HANA HANA HŪM PHAṬ

37. OM SVABHĀVA ŚHUDDHĀḤ SARVA DHARMĀḤ SVABHĀVA ŚHUDDHO HAM

38. Flowers, incense, lamps, scented water, and food.

39. That is, to recite it on a daily basis but not as your main practice.

40. A clear blue crystal or volcanic glass. Sometimes mistranslated as lapis lazuli.

41. The name of the wish-fulfilling tree.

42. A type of rock found in the Realm of the Thirty Three.

43. The fruit of the *Aegle marmelos* tree, also known as the Bengal quince, golden apple, stone apple, or wood apple.

44. Though Jamgön Kongrul does not specify which commentary exactly, this explanation of the accumulations is found in several commentaries on the Kalachakra tantra.

45. Disobedient unwholesome acts include eating after noon when you have vows not to, wearing jewelry when observing Mahayana sojong, and so forth. Such acts are not unwholesome by their nature, but doing them while you have vows against them is disobedient and disrespectful of the Buddha's words.

46. Here "the visible" refers to this lifetime.

47. *The Way of the Bodhisattva*, Chapter 2, verse 7ab.

48. The afflictive obscurations include the afflictions of greed, hatred, wrong view, and so forth, as well as their imprints. Cognitive obscurations include the dualistic apprehension of perceiver and perceived as separate. The obscurations to absorption are those obscurations that prevent one from attaining deep meditative states. They are sometimes also considered a type of cognitive absorption.

49. From *The King of Great Tantras, Glorious Guhyasamaja* (Skt. *Śrī Guhyasamaja Mahātantra Rāja*), Lhasa Kangyur vol. 81, p. 513b.

50. The first of the fourteen root downfalls of samaya is criticizing your vajra master.

51. Sakya Pandita, *Presentation of the Three Vows (sDom gsum rab dbye)*.

52. Two completion stage practices of the six yogas of Naropa. Tummo involves generating feelings of bliss and looking at their nature. Illusory body is meditating on the illusory nature of the body and all other forms.

53. The path of using practices involving the channels and winds, such as the six yogas of Naropa.

54. This refers to the eight traditions started by students of Pakmodrukpa, including the Drikung, Taklung, Tsalpa, and so forth.

55. The four characteristics are clarity, stability, pride of the deity, and power.

56. Three samadhis by which one achieves liberation: the samadhis of emptiness, the absence of attributes, and the absence of wishes.

57. At this point, the original includes Rangjung Dorje's *Single Heart Advice*. However that text is sealed for secrecy, and in consultation with Situ Rinpoche and Gyaltsap Rinpoche, His Holiness the Karmapa has asked that it not be included in this translation.

58. From *The Seven Points of Mind Training* by Ja Chekawa Yeshe Dorje.

59. *Letter to a Friend*, v. 29.

60. Lying about the highest human qualities means saying that you have qualities, powers, realizations, or achievements that you know you do not actually have.

61. The gurus and the Three Jewels.

62. After the first time, repeat the abbreviated form of the refuge prayer: We go for refuge to the great and glorious gurus. We go for refuge to the yidams, the gatherings of deities in the mandalas. We go for refuge to the bhagavan buddhas. We go for refuge to the True Dharma. We go for refuge to the noble sanghas. We go for refuge to the gatherings of heroes, dakinis, Dharma protectors, and guardians who have the eye of wisdom.

Glossary

AFFLICTIONS. The mental factors such as ignorance, desire, hatred, pride, wrong view, and so forth that disturb the mind and motivate negative actions.

AGGREGATES, FIVE. The five categories of physical form and mental events that we grasp at as being a single self or as belonging to a self. The five are form, feeling, conception, formation, and consciousness. They are also called the five aggregates of grasping.

AKSHOBHYA. One of the five buddhas of the five buddha families. Akshobhya's main activity is to purify karmic obscurations.

ĀLI AND KĀLI. The vowels and consonants of the Sanskrit alphabet, representing the sounds from which all speech and mantra derive.

APPROACH AND ACCOMPLISHMENT. Two phases of vajrayana deity practice.

ATISHA. The Indian scholar who brought the Kadampa lineage to Tibet.

BARDO. The period between death and the next rebirth when the consciousness of the deceased individual experiences various appearances which come from past karma.

BHUTAS. Harmful formless spirits.

CALM ABIDING. The meditation of resting the mind calmly and stably.

CREATION AND COMPLETION PHASES. Two phases of vajrayana practice. The emphasis of the creation phase is meditating on yidam deities to bring stability of mind. The completion phase consists of practices that entail effort such as the six yogas of Naropa and effortless practices such as mahamudra.

DEFEATS, FOUR. The violations that irrevocably break the vow of a bhikshu.

DHARANI. A form of mantra that is often quite long.

DHARMAKĀYA. See KAYAS.

DHYANA. A deep state of calm abiding meditation.

DÖN. A nonhuman spirit that causes illness.

ESSENCE KAYA. See KAYAS.

FIVE METHODS OF PLEASING. Five methods of pleasing the guru: service by massaging their feet, bathing them, voluntarily accepting whatever they say as a command, pleasing them in all ways with your acts, and properly doing what should be done and giving up what must not be done. Alternately, the five are offering whatever you have, listening to their commands, considering whatever they do good, considering whatever they say the truth, and continually supplicating them.

FONTANEL. The place on the crown of the head where three bones of the skull come together. Also called the Brahma aperture.

FOUNDATION VEHICLE. The initial teachings given by the Buddha to his disciples, which emphasize self-discipline and the lack of an individual self.

GAMPOPA. The master who combined the teachings of mind training from the Kadampa tradition with the mahamudra tradition of Milarepa. Many of the modern Kagyu traditions descend from Gampopa. 1079–1153.

HIGHER REALMS. The realms of humans and gods

ILLUSORY BODY. One of the six yogas of Naropa. This practice involves meditating on the illusory nature of the body and all other forms.

INSIGHT MEDITATION. Meditation on the true nature of phenomena.

KADAMPA. A Buddhist tradition stemming from Atisha and emphasizing the development of compassion through mind training. It was incorporated into the Kagyu tradition by Gampopa.

KARMA. Action. Our actions are all causes that will produce results in this or a future life.

KAYAS. The bodies of a buddha. The first is the dharmakaya, or body of qualities, which is the qualities of a buddha's wisdom, love, and power. As its essence is wisdom, it is only perceived by the buddhas. Since others cannot perceive the dharmakaya, buddhas manifest two different kinds of form kayas. The sambhogakaya, or enjoyment body, is visible to only those beings on high bodhisattva levels who have pure perception. The nirmanakaya, or emanation body, can be perceived by ordinary beings with impure perception. An example of a nirmanakaya would be Buddha Shakyamuni; an example of a sambhogakaya would be Avalokiteshvara. Sometimes the buddhas are also described as having a fourth kaya, the essence kaya (svabhavikakaya), which is described alternately as the union of the three kayas or as their empty nature.

LISTENER. A term for the Buddha's disciples of the Foundation Vehicle.

MAHAYANA. Literally, Great Vehicle. The second set of teachings given by the Buddha, which emphasize compassion and the lack of a self in phenomena.

MARAS. The demons who tempted the Buddha while he sat below the Bodhi tree. They represent the different types of attachment to samsara that obstruct spiritual practice.

NIRMANAKAYA. See KAYAS.

PRATYEKABUDDHA. A practitioner who awakens to nirvana without relying on a teacher in their last lifetime. Their realization is said to be greater than that of the listeners but less than a buddha's.

QUALITIES OF WATER, EIGHT. Sweet, cool, soft, light, pure, clean, not being harmful to the throat, and being beneficial to the stomach.

SAMADHI. Concentration and deep meditative states.

SAMAYA. The commitments of a practitioner of the secret mantra.

SAMBHOGAKAYA. See KAYAS.

SARVAVID. A form of the Buddha Vairochana, meditating upon which purifies obscurations that lead to the lower realms.

SIDDHA. A vajrayana adept who has accomplished high realization.

SIDDHIS. The powers that come from accomplishing the vajrayana path.

SPIRITUAL FRIEND. A term for a spiritual teacher frequently used in the context of the Mahayana.

TANTRAS. Teachings given by the buddhas in various forms at different times and locations. They generally emphasize methods for meditating to realize our inherent buddha nature. In the tradition of the Sarma (new translations), there are four classes of tantra: the action, conduct, yoga, and unexcelled yoga tantra. The unexcelled tantra also has three aspects: the father tantra which emphasizes means, the mother tantra which emphasizes wisdom, and the nondual tantras.

THREE SPHERES. The person performing the action, the recipient of the action, and the action itself.

TRANSCENDENCES, SIX. The six transcendent qualities of generosity, discipline, patience, diligence, dhyana, and wisdom. They are so called because they transcend ordinary, worldly generosity and so forth.

VAJRA POSTURE. A posture where the each foot rests on the opposite thigh. In the yoga tradition, this is called the full lotus posture.

VAJRA VARAHI. One of the principal yidam deities practiced in the Karma Kagyu tradition.

VAJRADHARA. The dharmakaya buddha, often portrayed with all the robes and ornaments of the sambhogakaya, blue in color and holding a vajra and bell in his crossed hands.

VOWS, THREE TYPES OF. The pratimoksha vows such as the lay precepts or monastic vows, the bodhisattva vows, and the tantric vows or samaya.

WORLDLY CONCERNS, EIGHT. Being pleased with gain, fame, praise, and the pleasant, and being displeased with loss, obscurity, criticism, and the unpleasant.

YIDAM. A meditational deity.

May All Beings Be Happy